JULIA ROBERTS

America's Sweetheart

BY **MARK BEGO**

Edited by Nicholas Maier

American Media, Inc.

JULIA ROBERTS
America's Sweetheart

Copyright © 2003 AMI Books, Inc.

Cover design: Carlos Plaza
Interior design: Debbie Browning

ISBN: 1-932270-09-4

First printing: July 2003

Printed in the United States of America

10 9 8 7 6 5 4 3 2 1

INTRODUCTION

America's Sweetheart

For the past two decades, Julia Roberts has been rated as one of the most talented and most versatile actresses in Hollywood. Ever since the late 1980s, when her trademark smile and her effervescent charm first delighted movie fans around the world, she has been a bona fide star. With performances in more than 30 films, Julia is known as everyone's favorite *Pretty Woman*. An

Academy Award and multiple Golden Globe winner, she has sealed her place as one of the most beloved actresses in film history.

Now in the 21st century, Julia's films have collectively grossed more than $2 billion worldwide, making her one of the top all-time box-office drawing women in cinema's past century. Not surprisingly, she is now the highest-paid female in movie history. Her asking price for starring in a film is currently an astronomical $20 million. She was paid that amount for both *Erin Brockovich* and *The Mexican*. However, if a good script comes around, like her brief-but-memorable featured role in *Ocean's Eleven* and her mysterious appearance in *Confessions of a Dangerous Mind*, she has been known to cut her fee in half to take a paltry $10 million.

Although Julia excels at portraying the perky girl-next-door, as she has in *Pretty Woman, My Best Friend's Wedding* and *Steel Magnolias*, Julia is always up for a challenge. She isn't afraid to tackle darker roles—like the terrified mad-scientist's maid in *Mary Reilly*, or the rebel's dour girlfriend in *Michael Collins*. While she's most famous for her string of light comedies, she can also play more dramatic roles. The thrilling *The*

Pelican Brief and the touching *Stepmom* cemented her ability to portray more serious characters as successfully as she handles her trademark exuberant comedies.

In the 2000 film hit *Erin Brockovich*, Julia truly struck cinematic gold. She was so compelling and believable as the unconventional and fiery "people's rights" champion that she received her third Academy Award nomination. In March 2001, Julia Roberts won the Best Actress trophy for her touching and amusing portrayal as the real-life Brockovich. But in spite of her dozens of films, she is still best known for her role as Vivian, the hooker, in the sparkling 1990 comedy *Pretty Woman*. Co-starring with Richard Gere in this magical Cinderella tale made her an international sensation.

Not only is she vastly popular with her fans and the public in general, but she is also a big hit with her leading men as well. She has played opposite some of the most dashing and most famous actors in the movie business, including Hugh Grant, Liam Neeson, Dennis Quaid, John Malkovich, Kiefer Sutherland, Denzel Washington, Nick Nolte, George Clooney, Brad Pitt, Matt Damon, Rupert Everett, Ed Harris, James Gandolfini, Blair Underwood, John Cusack and Woody Allen.

Julia's personal life, however, is a confusing dichotomy that runs both hot and cold, and her lovers have been a patchwork of more than a dozen men. Ever since she was a teenager, she has been known to be a "serial dater" with a life-long habit of falling in love with the handsome leading men of her films, having hot and heavy affairs, and then tossing the men by the wayside. On one hand she is known for her warmth and friendliness, yet she has another side as well. When she is finished with a relationship, she has the ability to instantly terminate that man from her life with icy precision. Only once has one of her high-profile boyfriends dumped her first.

Julia Roberts' past is littered with suitors, boyfriends, fiancés and lovers. She is known as something of a heartbreaker. Her list of "A" list beaus includes Liam Neeson, Kiefer Sutherland, Lyle Lovett, Benjamin Bratt, Matthew Perry, Daniel Day-Lewis, Jason Patric and Dylan McDermott. There is even a rumored fling with John F. Kennedy Jr. in the early 1990s. But her conquests are not limited to famous actors alone. Her former boyfriends have included bartenders and personal trainers as well.

As the year 2003 began, oddsmakers were betting on how many more months her recent marriage to cameraman Danny Moder would last. Lyle Lovett, the only other man to rise to the title of husband with Julia, made it only two years before being given the ax. With her set pattern of stopping a relationship in an instant, it seemed only a matter of time. She truly is becoming the embodiment of one of her most famous films, *Runaway Bride*.

In addition to the mystery of Julia's love life is her controversial relationship with her own family. She literally owes her first big break to older brother Eric Roberts. And, like Eric had done for her, Julia has often insisted that her sister Lisa be cast in her films and television projects. Lisa can be spotted in Julia's episode of *Friends*, as well as in films like *Something to Talk About* and *I Love Trouble*. Julia remains close to her mother, Betty, and her sister Lisa. However, she has not spoken to Eric in more than 10 years and their bitter feud carries on today.

Regardless of the fact that Julia has one of the most glamorous lives in Hollywood today, it is interesting to note that she doesn't personally think of herself as a glamour queen.

"That's one of my aspirations," she claims. "I would love to be elegant, but I don't think I am. I guess we all want to be Audrey Hepburn." At one time, her sudden fame embarrassed her. "Well, I've learned to accept a compliment," she reveals. "I've learned how to say 'thank you,' but I also realize that I'm not in high school anymore. If someone compliments me, it doesn't send me swooning."

She is also modest about her beauty. "I have good posture, I'd have to say that," she shyly admits.

So what is the real-life Julia Roberts all about? Is she a spoiled diva or a modest regular girl? Behind the million-watt smile, is she really happy? Like the *Runaway Bride*, Julia, too, has left behind her a trail of broken hearts. She pursues them, possesses them and then shows them the door. What is it that really makes her tick? Three times on the screen, Julia has played the role of a mother. Is she ever going to do it in real life or is she too devoted to her career?

To solve the riddle of Julia Roberts, and to answer all of these questions, one has to go all the way back to the small town of Smyrna, Georgia, where it all began.

CHAPTER ONE

Smyrna, Georgia

ocated just northwest of Atlanta, in the Peachtree State of Georgia, Smyrna isn't exactly the most likely birthplace for a glamorous movie star. But for Julie Fiona Roberts, that's where it all began. It wasn't until she began her professional acting career that she changed the spelling of her first name from "Julie" to "Julia."

The third child of Walter and Betty Roberts, Julie came into the world Oct. 28, 1967. Her older brother, Eric was born April 18, 1956, in Biloxi, Mississippi, where the family lived before they moved to Smyrna. Julie's arrival was preceded by two years by her older sister Lisa.

"I was really influenced by my family," recalls Julia, touching upon how all the Roberts children grew up to become professional actors. "My parents had a theater school in Piedmont Park in Atlanta, though it was pretty much over by the time I could walk and talk and formulate my thoughts. There are pictures from that time of me playing in the dirt next to the stage while they're working. Being exposed to that environment must have had an effect on me, because as a young person I used to come up with these wild fantasies. I had one about Vincent van Gogh. Apparently he was entranced with a woman named Ursula and he'd walk miles and miles just to watch her leave her house to go to church. So I'd come up with these scenarios where I was the reincarnation of Ursula and van Gogh was in love with me."

As a young child, Julia got to see first hand how theater and acting didn't always make stable careers. Although artistically fulfilling, they were often low paying. The Roberts' theater workshop was—as one report described it—"a financial disaster."

Julia recalls watching her parents occasionally struggle and how it taught her some valuable lessons. "My dad ended up selling vacuum cleaners and my mom got a job as a secretary. They never got rich and they never got famous, but they showed me that you do things for a purpose, and that if it treats you well, then all the better. But if it goes away, you won't die. You just move on."

In spite of money problems, Julia remembers her home life as being very warm and loving when she was growing up in Georgia. "I come from a real touchy family. A lotta hugging, a lotta kissing, a lotta love: 'You're going to the market? See you later, I love you.' And it's funny to bring that outside of the Roberts house and into the real world."

Thinking back to her early days in Smyrna, Julia fondly recalls, "I was raised by parents that believed in love and peace and happiness and flowers and all those things, and I still believe in them."

She also recalls feeling very awkward as a child. "Growing up," Julia explains, "I didn't excel at anything. I wasn't particularly scholarly, I wasn't particularly athletic, I wasn't particularly attractive. I was sort of just very average and mediocre. I didn't have anything to claim for myself, to say, 'This is what

I am—I am the student, I am the athlete.' I didn't have a claim to stake."

However, it wasn't long before the idea of becoming an actress started to appeal to her. In addition to loving stage acting, Julia grew up fascinated with the movies. When she is asked what her favorite movie is, she replies, "Now, *Voyager*. I love that movie. I also love *The Philadelphia Story* and *The Nun's Story*. *Becket* was a huge influence on me. I saw it in high school and it really put me over the top in terms of making me want to make movies."

Recalling the music that she used to listen to when she was a child, Julia says, "Growing up I liked Louis Armstrong. And being from the South, I just thought the Atlanta Rhythm Section, .38 Special and Bad Company were the greatest bands ever. But when I moved to New York, no one there knew what I was talking about when I said I liked .38 Special."

In 1971, money problems and several other pressures reportedly broke the Roberts' marriage up, leaving a trail of hurt feelings. All three children lived with their mother, Betty. In 1972 she remarried. Her new husband was a journalist by the name of Michael Motes. It wasn't long before battle lines were drawn, especially between Eric and his new stepfather. When one of their arguments turned into a fist fight, Betty threw Eric out of the house and he went to live with his father.

Walter Roberts moved in with a sexy looking neighbor by the name of Eileen Sellars right after the divorce was final, and they were married in 1974. As with many cases of divorce, things turned ugly and a custody battle between Betty and Walter ensued. At one point, Walter allegedly planted drugs at Betty's house and called the police on her.

An ugly family life turned tragic. In 1977, Eric was out canoeing with stepmother Eileen, when she fell into the water and drowned. At the same time, Walter was struggling with throat cancer. Three months after Eileen died, Walter lost his battle with cancer. All three Roberts children were understandably affected by the sudden and heart-wrenching loss.

Julia was just 9 years old at the time. "His death changed the course of my life and at some point or other has altered every philosophy of life I've ever had," she sadly claims.

She remembers her father with a great sense of fondness. "I had a great relationship with my dad," she says. "Nothing intellectual, just really caring and fun, singing the *Oompa-Loompas* song or drawing and painting."

When the subject of Walter Roberts comes up, Julia reminisces, "I miss my dad. I don't feel that boundless injustice over his death anymore, which is good, because that's not a fun bag to carry. It was just something that happened to me. It's funny that I said that: that was really a selfish thing to say. His death happened to a lot of people. But when I was 9 years old, it felt like this was done to me. Now I look at it as: I can talk to him whenever I want, he's everywhere I go."

According to her, the tragedy made her long to one day have a family of her own. "I think it would be great to have a big family, to get together with our kids, who have kids," she was later to daydream out loud.

Although Walter Roberts had no money of his own at the time of his death, Eileen had left him $100,000 and made Eric the executor of the will. He was also made responsible for his sister's share of the will. This led to a strain-filled court battle between Betty Roberts and her son Eric. She launched into a reported 18-month lawsuit to get Julia and Lisa's share of their father's money away from Eric's control. She eventually won and Julia's $25,000 was put into a trust fund for her when she was 12 years old, but the seeds of family bitterness had been firmly planted.

When Julia was a teenager, she began classes at local Campbell High School. According to some reports, she was very frustrated with her homelife, as she never really cared for her stepfather. According to her classmates, Julia was very popular in school. Her winning smile was already her calling card, even then.

One of her boyfriends back then was Jeff Hardigree. He recalls, "Julia was boy crazy in high school. I was a football star and she was hot for jocks. Guys were especially attractive to her if they already had girlfriends. She was a 15-year-old sophomore and was a friend of my girlfriend Lisa—but she set her sights on me immediately."

According to Hardigree, her ploy worked and he dated Julia off and on for more than a year. Disappointed, Jeff explained, "But then it became apparent that it wasn't me she was interested in. I realized she saw me as just another conquest."

Herbie Holder, who was on the baseball team at Campbell High School, claims that Julia was infatuated with the jocks who played baseball, basketball and football. He claims, "When the baseball season came around, we had batting practice—and Julia Roberts—she was always hanging around. It was the same in the football and basketball seasons. Julia always followed the sports stars.

We had a special nickname for her: "Hot Pants Roberts."

Many of the girls she went to school with felt like they had to watch out for man-stealing Julia. Even then, she was a notorious flirt. Another of her classmates revealed of Julia, "She pretended to be my best friend and all the while she was telephoning my boyfriend behind my back."

At a Saturday night party, Miss Roberts reportedly moved in for the kill. Says the same classmate, "We were all having a great time, dancing and drinking vodka and Coke. Then Julia maneuvered my boyfriend off into a dark corner and started kissing him. The next thing I knew they'd disappeared and I was left to find my way home alone. She stole my boyfriend. I was ready to scratch her eyes out."

According to the classmate, Julia came to her senior prom solo, then spent the evening seeing whose boyfriend she could steal away. "She dressed like a vamp that night and batted her eyes and wiggled her hips at every guy in the room. Julia sent out vibes that she was available. All the other girls were disgusted by her behavior."

Another classmate who was at the prom, Kelly Rice, sourly recalls, "She latched onto my boyfriend and made a big play for him—even though she could clearly see I was his date. He and I had a row over her. I couldn't get rid of her! In the end, I had to drag him away and tell her to get lost."

Claimed Kelly, "[Julia] changed boyfriends as often as she changed underwear."

The next event that followed Julia's senior prom was her high school graduation. It would also very quickly signify her escape from Smyrna, Georgia. It wasn't going to be long before "Hot Pants Roberts" was going to move on to bigger and better things. However, her life-long pattern for jumping from boyfriend to boyfriend was already set.

One of the most destiny-shaping things that had happened in Julia's young life was watching her older brother Eric launch his own successful acting career. It was in 1978, the year that Julia turned 11, that Eric Roberts' first major film, *King of the Gypsies*, was released. One of his co-stars in this film was an actress by the name of Susan Sarandon. Ironically, Sarandon was later to become one of Julia's best friends and film co-stars in the 1990s.

In rapid succession, Eric proceeded to build his love for acting into a very successful film career. During the next couple of years, he was to be one of the stars of films including *Raggity Man* (1981), *Star 80* (1983) and *The Pope of Greenwich Village* (1984).

Observing her brother's meteoric rise to fame as a movie star, it wasn't long before Julia had her own heart set on the idea of acting in movies. "I don't want it to seem like I was doing it just because the others were. But there comes a time when you have to own up to what's pulling you," she says.

By the time she was a teenager, she recalls the feeling that she had been "restless without focus." Trying to explain the emotion further, she says, "A friend of mine gave me a great image: There's a bottle full of beads and you want to pour all the beads out. I used to feel that urgency, that anxiety, like something's going to break. I still feel that sometimes, but for different reasons than I did when I was 17 and wanted to leave Georgia."

She was so restless, in fact, she moved to New York City three days after her high school graduation. She felt that she didn't want to waste a moment of time. "College wasn't for me," she remembers. "I couldn't see bolting out of bed at 8 o'clock to be 10 minutes late for some f***ing class with some f***ing guy who's just gonna stick it to me again."

Julia headed straight to Manhattan, to her sister Lisa's apartment in Greenwich Village. It was 1986 and for a while, Julia played with the idea of being a model.

She then switched her focus back to acting. Taking acting classes seemed like a good idea to her, but as she explains, "I always quit the classes. Halfway through I thought, 'This guy's full of s**t.' " She was headstrong even then. However, it was all about to pay off for her. Her lucky break was right around the corner.

CHAPTER TWO

Aspiring Actress

Living with her sister Lisa in New York City, Julia's career didn't seem to be taking off as quickly as she thought it might. Fortunately, it was her brother Eric who came to the rescue. He had just been cast in a new film called *Blood Red*. Upon his suggestion, the producers of the film auditioned her and she was given her very first movie role. Although the movie was filmed in 1986, it was not released until 1988, when it went straight to video.

Based on the title alone, *Blood Red* seems like it should be a teenage slasher flick. Instead it is a tale about the struggles of a group of Italian vineyard owners in late 1880s California. The star of the film is Eric Roberts as Marco Collogero, the son of a vineyard owner, proud Italian immigrant Sebastian Collogero (Giancarlo Giannini). Dennis Hopper plays evil railroad owner William Bradford Berrigan and Burt Young—of *Rocky* fame—is Berrigan's murderous henchman, Andrews.

Julia portrays the role of Marco's younger sister, Maria. It is such a small part that she isn't even mentioned in the opening credits.

Unfortunately, much of this film is bogged down in dialogue. Other parts of it are simply violent and bloody—hence the name of the film. Although, Eric's sex scenes are fun to watch, if only as sheer camp. A movie about injustice and brutality reigning over diplomacy, *Blood Red* is a bloody bore to watch. It can't seem to decide whether to be a romance novel brought to life or a historical film. It doesn't succeed very well on either count. However, as her first film role, Julia proved that she has a great on-camera presence and that she could indeed act. *Blood Red*'s biggest claim to fame will always be as "Julia Roberts' film debut."

The next film that Julia was cast in was

called *Firehouse*. It was a teenage exploitation film with all of the seriousness of, say, *Police Academy*. About the sexual goings-on in a firehouse, it is cut from the same cloth of another epic from the era: *Porky's*. Julia Roberts can be briefly spotted amidst the action, as Babs. In a cast full of actors who would remain unknown, Julia is the only person from *Firehouse* whose career turned into anything of note. And, to say that she eclipsed the rest of the cast in *Firehouse* is a bit of an understatement. It is such an obscure film that it is no longer available on either VHS or DVD.

Video Guide 2001 by Mick Martin and Marsha Porter best describes *Firehouse* as "*Charlie's Angels* clone set in a firehouse"—recommended for Julia Roberts junkies only.

Giving her career another dimension, Julia also landed roles on two television series.

On the program called *Crime Story*, a series dealing with police detectives in the early 1960s, she was seen portraying the role of "Tracy" in an episode called "The Survivor," broadcast Feb. 13, 1987. During the run of the show, several people, who were soon-to-be-stars, appeared on *Crime Story*, including Christian Slater, Ving Rhames, David Hyde-

Pierce, Kevin Spacey, cult film star Pam Grier (*Jackie Brown*) and, of course, Julia.

In 1988, Julia Roberts was seen in another popular TV series, *Miami Vice*. She played the part of "Polly Wheeler" on the episode entitled "Mirror Image." It was first broadcast May 6, 1988.

Along with these series appearances, Julia also landed roles in a pair of films that were originally produced for television. The first one was a film made for the HBO television network entitled *Baja Oklahoma*.

In *Baja Oklahoma* Julia plays the role of Candy, who is the teenage daughter of Juanita Hutchins (Lesley Ann Warren), a waitress and bartender at Herb's Bar & Grill. When her old flame, Slick Henderson (Peter Coyote) returns to town and comes back into her life, he inspires her to pursue her dreams of becoming a professional songwriter.

Baja Oklahoma is a light comic film, with some very funny moments. This is not a brilliant film, but it is an enjoyable one, which gave Julia the opportunity to shine in her scenes with Lesley Ann Warren.

Leonard Maltin's Movie & Video Guide calls *Baja Oklahoma* a "lively adaptation of Dan Jenkins' funny novel of a smalltime

Texas barmaid ... loaded with local color ... above average."

Julia's next made-for-TV movie was one called *Satisfaction*. For a low-budget rock 'n' roll movie, *Satisfaction* is quite fun to watch. It is the story of an all-girl band, Jennie Lee & The Mystery, and their one big summer. They land a gig in a small beach community and their shot at finding rock star fame. The band is led by Jennie Lee (Justine Bateman), the film's biggest star at the time. She had just become a household name for her role on TV's *Family Ties*, and this was one of her shots at turning her television fame into a successful movie career.

When Jennie Lee & The Mystery audition for a summer gig at a beach club called Falcon's, they win over the club owner (Liam Neeson) with their performance.

Julia is fascinating to watch, playing tough girl Daryle. Of her first three films, this is the one that stands out and features Julia at her most entertaining and appealing. She enlivens all of her dialogue, taking a line as mundane as "Let's make breakfast!" and turns it into a high-wattage statement. She looks great as she delivers tons of attitude in her torn jeans and leather jacket.

One of the biggest things to happen to Julia during the filming of *Satisfaction* was that she began an affair with her film co-star, Liam Neeson. Their love affair only lasted from 1987 to 1988 and both of them went on to other things. Her fling with the older Neeson set up a pattern that was going to become a recurring theme throughout her career.

CHAPTER THREE

Overnight Sensation

Finally, after four feature films and guest starring roles on two popular crime-drama television series, Julia landed the movie role that was going to take her from the career stage of "aspiring actress" to "star-in-the-making." It was a modest but fun teenage female bonding film that takes place in the fishing port of Mystic, Connecticut. It was called *Mystic Pizza*.

At the time that this film was made, it was intended to be a vehicle to launch the film stardom of another aspiring young actress, Annabeth Gish. However, when it was released—and from that point forward—it became famous for being the film that made Julia Roberts a star.

Mystic Pizza is a totally entertaining teenage movie, with a little bit of everything in it: comedy, tragedy, sex and a happy ending.

When it was released in October 1988, the reviews were very good. The most clairvoyant comment of all came from Roger Ebert in *The Chicago Sun-Times*, when he perceptively proclaimed, "I have a feeling that *Mystic Pizza* may someday become known for the movie stars it showcased back before they became stars. All of the young actors in this movie have genuine gifts. Roberts is a major beauty with a fierce energy."

Because of her success in *Mystic Pizza*, Roberts was suddenly a recognizable star. Her fame was still so new to her that it often led to amusing incidents. According to Julia, "One time, I had gone to the movies with my mother in Georgia and I was in the bathroom. All of a sudden this voice says, 'Excuse me. The girl in stall number one. Were you in *Mystic Pizza*?' I said, 'Yeah,' she goes, 'Can I have your autograph?' and slides a piece of paper under the stall door. I just said, 'I don't think right now is the time.'"

The next film that Julia Roberts appeared in was going to become an even more important step for her in her growing film career. It was a well-written character-driven play about a group of women in the South, called *Steel Magnolias*. It was written by Robert Harling and it started out as a highly successful play in Greenwich Village. Its evolution is a fascinating story in itself.

"I have one of those very close-knit, completely unique Southern families," explains native Louisiana writer Robert Harling. "And I had a younger sister named Susan who was not just a sister, but my best friend. We lived sort of, I guess, normal, but had a somewhat eccentric family. And she got married and she wanted a child. She really, really wanted a child very badly. And she was advised, that because of the nature of her condition, that it might be a little risky. But, she went ahead and said, 'I'm going to have a kid.' And then, shortly after, she started to have some complications. And, the complications unfortunately led to her death. This was a very, very, very painful thing for me. I was living in New York. I was sort of separated from the family. I was having a lot of anger. I was having a really hard time with it. And, some friends of mine, one of whom was a play-wright and his wife, advised me, they said, 'Write something about it.' There was this child ... and his mother, who was the most wonderful person I'd ever known, had basi-cally given her life so that this child would exist. And, he would never know what she was about. He would never know what a wonderful human being she was ... I decided I would write a short story for him. And, as I began to write the short story, the form didn't seem quite right. So, I started writing a play. And I thought it was going to be a one act, but by the time it was finished, it wasn't a one-act, it was a full play." This became the play called *Steel Magnolias*.

Continues Harling, "The nature of this play, particularly, was very dramatic, because it was sealed in the idea of a beauty parlor, where a sense of community existed between these women that came to literally let their hair down. When you are able to shoot a film, you have the license and free-dom to go and see all of the events which are just discussed. Because in the play, these women would bring in all the stories of their lives and share them with the other women. Now we have the advantage of going and watching those lives and seeing how these women are impacted by their families and how that resonates in the community of women in the beauty shop."

Casting these very colorful women was one of the most creative aspects of bringing *Steel Magnolias* to the screen. Dolly Parton, Shirley MacLaine, Sally Field and Daryl Hannah had already been hired for their parts, but the actress to play the crucial role of Shelby had yet to be found. According to Harling, "I think when we were casting, we had this amazing cast and we were still looking for the role of sister. And [producer] Herbert [Ross] said, 'I just saw somebody today, and I think she's magic.' I'm very proprietary of the role, because that is my sister we are talking about. She walks in and it's as if someone has turned up the lights a little bit. And I said, 'Oh, that's her!' "

Shirley MacLaine claims of Julia, "The moment she walked on the set for the first rehearsal, I called my agent and said, 'I think you should handle her. This girl's going to be a star.' And we hadn't even done one scene."

According to Harling, "Julia approached the role with such sincerity and such passion that I could tell something really special was happening."

Julia was an instant hit on the *Magnolias* set. Says Sally Field, "The minute I met her, I wanted to wrap my arms around her. But at the same time, she's got a kind of toughness."

Of *Steel Magnolias* director Herb Ross, Sally claimed, "Herb is a good director, but in some ways he was extremely hard on Julia. We all felt it was uncalled for, but she's a warrior."

Ross admitted, "I'm a taskmaster. I never spoke privately to anyone: If I had criticism or advice, I would say it in front of the other women. And Julia worked hard. She stayed in bed for the coma scenes eight, twelve hours a day, until she was ill and dizzy."

One of the most dramatic sequences in the film surrounds Shelby having a diabetic attack in the beauty parlor. Herbert Ross explains, "I talked to the local hospital and asked Bob [Harling] at great length what would happen when his sister would succumb to these. So, once we had the general knowledge what occurred, I left it to Julia to make those discoveries. I mean I can say, 'you do this ... you do that,' you know, and she filled it in. It looks very effective still and very convincing."

Steel Magnolias is a very well done, touching, funny and ultimately winning film.

Among the keys to its success is a strong script and an incredible cast.

Just as Julia had during the filming of *Satisfaction*, while she was making *Steel Magnolias*, she ended up dating one of the cast members. This time around it was handsome Dylan McDermott, who played her husband in the film. Their romance blossomed very quickly and suddenly the couple announced their engagement. However, their affair only lasted from 1988 to 1989, when Julia suddenly broke it off. This was going to become a habit for her during the next couple of years.

Released Nov. 5, 1989, when the reviews came out for *Steel Magnolias*, the media unanimously heralded the major-feature film arrival of Julia Roberts. They raved about how she was able to hold her own next to five such accredited female stars. Peter Travers of *Rolling Stone* loved *Steel Magnolias*, pointing out, "No use fighting it. This laugh-getting, tear-jerking, part-affecting, part-appalling display of audience manipulation is practically critic-proof ... producer Ray Stark and director Herbert Ross have wisely hired the luminous likes of Sally Field, Dolly Parton, Shirley MacLaine, Daryl Hannah, Olympia Dukakis and Julia Roberts. The result can best be described as shamelessly entertaining. Field has the key role of the self-sacrificing mother who would do anything, even donate a kidney, to save her sick daughter, played by Roberts (actor Eric's radiant sister) ... The ladies are live wires. Just stand back and watch them set off sparks."

In *The Chicago Sun-Times*, Roger Ebert found, "*Steel Magnolias* is essentially a series of comic one-liners leading up to a teary tragedy, but let it be said that the one-liners are mostly funny and the tragedy deserves most, but not all, of the tears ... wonderfully entertaining performances from all of the women in his cast ... The principal pleasure of the movie is in the ensemble work of the actresses, as they trade one-liners and zingers and stick together and dish the dirt."

Steel Magnolias was so popular that it grossed more than $85 million at the box office in North America alone. In addition to her critical success, Julia was nominated for a Golden Globe Award by the Foreign Press Association for her portrayal of Shelby. Much to her surprise, as she sat in her seat during the ceremony, she heard the presenter calling out her name as the winner.

The night of the Golden Globe Awards was
one that Julia will always remember.
According to her, "I have to say the Golden
Globes was the most shocking night of my
life. I was so unprepared. I heard a recording
of my acceptance speech later and I had to
laugh. I was such an idiot."

When the Academy Award nominations
were announced in early 1990, Julia's performance in *Steel Magnolias* was on the list
in the category of Best Supporting Actress. It
was like a dream come true for her, to be
nominated at the young age of 22. According
to her, "It feels like it does when you're walking around on a hot summer day and all of a
sudden it starts to rain really hard—it's cold
and it feels good, and it makes you want to
dance around. And then it stops and you
keep on walking." Ultimately, it was Whoopi
Goldberg who won the Best Supporting
Actress Oscar that year, for her role in the
film *Ghost*. However, the whole world now
knew that Julia Roberts had arrived—in a
very big way.

Julia looks back on this era with fondness.
Proclaiming how she maintains her equilibri-
um amidst stardom, she says, "Part of it is that
I've had the same core circle of friends since

before I was famous. And most of them aren't actors. I'm the same person to them whether I have a successful movie or not. I think that might have something to do with it."

Julia's career was booming. Magazines were doing cover stories on her and featuring her in fashion spreads. She was also literally deluged with film offers. Julia said at the time that the biggest challenge she was facing was no longer getting film offers, it was maintaining her perspective as her star rose. She admitted that it was a constant struggle to maintain her equilibrium. "The most difficult thing in the world is to be simple, to reduce things down to simple terms," she explained in 1990. "There are times when Hollywood is very unattractive to me. But there was a time in New York when I had nothing but time on my hands—and when Hollywood has no charm and everyone just wants you, you have to be grateful and remember the times you were sitting in your apartment with nothing to do."

CHAPTER FOUR

Pretty Woman

*S*uddenly, Julia Roberts was so popular that she entered a hectic phase of her career where she would film one movie and then immediately go on to the next one. Things were going very fast for her, as producers and directors competed to work with her. While *Steel Magnolias* was still in post-production, she was busy on her next film—a comedy called *Pretty Woman*.

Explaining how she selects her movie roles, Julia once stated, "They seem to choose me, not the other way around."

However, when she found out about *Pretty Woman* being cast, she claims that it was a role she "chased down like a dog." Speaking of the character of Vivian in *Pretty Woman*, Julia explained, "I just loved her. My reaction to her was a balance of intrigue and fear—the same balance I felt toward Daisy in *Mystic Pizza* and Shelby in *Steel Magnolias*."

It was amusing that the film was produced by the adult division of the highly G-rated Disney Corporation—here she was, cast in her first Disney movie and she was playing a Hollywood Boulevard prostitute. How was she going to break the news to her mother? Recalls Julia, "My mom works for the Catholic archdiocese of Atlanta. I mean my mom's boss baptized me! So I called her at work and it was like, 'Hi Mom, I got a job.' She said, 'You did! What'd you get?' And I said, 'Oh, it's a Disney movie. I gotta go. I'll talk to you later.' "

Director Garry Marshall found Julia to actually be quite fragile and shy at the beginning of filming *Pretty Woman*. "When we started the picture, she was a little scared," he revealed. "Her body language sort of said, 'I don't want to be the center of attention.' But she couldn't help it."

According to Marshall, he uses different techniques for getting the best performances out of each of his actors. "We try to shoot each performer differently," he claims. "And, the approach for Julia—quite honestly—is that we shoot her like Bambi. She moves around, Julia. She never quite stands still. You just kinda sorta see her and that's the way we shot her. She's there, she's beautiful—bam, she's gone. We kidded about it: 'All right, we're doing Bambi in the Penthouse today!'"

Garry found that one of Julia's most stunning attributes were her legs. He described them as "possibly the longest legs since Wilt Chamberlain." According to him, "Even when Julia is being schlumpy, she's schlumpy with elegance."

Instantly Marshall realized that the way to get the best and most subtle performances out of Julia, he had to make sure the on-set climate was absolutely perfect. "She performs well when loved," he claims. "Richard Gere and I took great pains to try and make her feel comfortable and make her feel loved and make it a pleasant experience—not because we're such nice people, but because that was the best thing for the project. The dramatic moments where she was going to be very vulnerable were very hard for her. You're with a guy like Richard Gere for six or seven weeks and suddenly you do this scene where he screams in your face and yells at you. And it hurts her. He's used to that, but she was devastated in that scene. After each take she was crying and we'd have to hold her a moment to make sure she was all right. That's her word process and you have to understand that and be supportive. And the other area of her vulnerability was the scene where she had to talk about her father. I didn't ask her about that, but I could see she was touchy. So I just held her in between takes of those scenes and then she was fine."

Looking back at Julia Roberts' entire career, *Mystic Pizza* will be known as the film in which audiences truly discovered her. *Steel Magnolias* will be remembered as the film that made her a movie star. But, it is *Pretty Woman* that will forever be thought of as the film that made her an international superstar.

Here she was in 1990, becoming a huge box-office star by playing a hooker in *Pretty Woman*. Ironically, it was exactly 10 years previous that Richard Gere, too, became a huge star playing a boy-for-rent in the title role in *American Gigolo*. Between the two of them, the sex appeal factor in this movie was one of the keys to its success.

The story has a very cute premise to it. As someone who has had a lousy time sustaining relationships, Edward Lewis (Richard Gere) picks up a Hollywood Boulevard hooker named Vivian Ward. Initially, all he wanted was driving directions to Beverly Hills. However, one thing leads to another and she escorts him back to his luxurious suite at the Regency Beverly Wilshire Hotel. Well, companionship turns to sex, sex turns to love and with love comes the complications.

One of Julia's most bewitching segments of the film surrounds her Cinderella transformation. Her first venture to the shops in the Rodeo Drive vicinity proves a disaster. Saleswomen openly insult her hookeresque outfit. Later in the film, she has her own Audrey Hepburn-inspired trying-on-clothes fashion segment, as Edward takes her to a chic store and proceeds to drop "an obscene amount of money" on Vivian's new wardrobe.

One of the most memorable scenes in the film is the one where Richard Gere presents Julia with a stunning ruby and diamond necklace to wear to an important dinner. Recalls Garry Marshall, "We're shooting this scene and it's nice but not special. So I pull Richard aside and say, 'Snap the lid of the box on her fingers to surprise her when she reaches for the necklace.' Now, in that situation, she could get annoyed, she could make a remark, but instead she burst out laughing. Audiences loved her for that."

There's lots of sexy scenes between Gere and Roberts—in bed, in the bathtub, back in bed. There's also some humorously delightful scenes of them out in public. At a polo match, Vivian tells one of Edward's snooty female friends, "I'm not trying to 'land' him, I'm just using him for sex."

As Edward gets used to having streetwise-but-innocent Vivian around, he begins to shape her into his vision of what a lady should be. Through all of its plot twists, like all good fairy tales, *Pretty Woman* ultimately delivers a happily-ever-after ending.

Julia is extremely charming and playful as Vivian. It is obvious from the start that her brittle exterior hides a vulnerable soul within. That is a very big part of her allure. She was positively endearing in *Pretty Woman* and she sold cinema tickets like hotcakes.

When it was released in March 1990, critics unanimously loved *Pretty Woman* and overwhelmingly saluted Julia Roberts' performance. Deeson Howe in *The Washington Post* wrote, "It's Roberts' memorably comic performance that is the most distinguishing aspect of the movie. As the gawky professional companion, she's ticklishly appealing; on one occasion she accidentally projects an escargot through the air at a strategic dinner meeting and, at that opera visit, innocently declares, 'There's a band!' "

In that same newspaper, Rita Kempley wrote, "Julia Roberts and Richard Gere co-star in this bubbly scamper, which goes to the head like champagne ... and Roberts is sheer carbonation. An Oscar nominee for her role in *Steel Magnolias*, she is as exuberant as a cheerleader in the role of streetwise Vivian Ward ... *Pretty Woman* seduces all but the most wary. That's because the lady is a tramp."

Roger Ebert of *The Chicago Sun-Times* claimed, "It's the sweetest and most open-hearted love fable since *The Princess Bride* ... it glows with romance ... Roberts does an interesting thing; she gives her character an irrepressibly bouncy sense of humor and then lets her spend the movie trying to repress it. Actresses who can do that and look great can have whatever they want in Hollywood."

In early 1991, when the Academy Award

nominations were announced, Julia Roberts was up for one of the trophies in the Best Actress category for her portrayal of Vivian, though she did not take home an Oscar. However, she was honored to be considered an Academy Award-worthy actress—for the second time—at the young age of 23. In addition to being nominated for an American Academy Award, she was also nominated for a trophy in the same category at the British Academy Awards. And she won her second Golden Globe Award in the category of Best Actress (Musical or Comedy).

Pretty Woman was so popular that it became one of the 15 top films of all time and when it was released on video, it became the most rented video ever. By January 1991, it was also the biggest grossing movie in Disney's history, taking in more than $178 million domestically and $184 internationally.

The honors kept rolling in when in the September 1990 issue of *Harper's Bazaar*, Julia was featured in a fashion spread entitled "America's 10 Most Beautiful Women." The other women that Roberts shared the spread with included Shirley MacLaine, Winona Ryder, Andie MacDowell, Farrah Fawcett, Janet Jackson and Isabella Rossellini.

A busy and rising superstar before *Pretty Woman* was even released, Julia had already started on her next film—the thriller *Flatliners*. Director Joel Schumacher recalls, "The first time Julia came to my house to discuss *Flatliners*, she was barefoot, wearing cutoff jeans and no makeup, and I thought, 'If she decides not to do my movie, I'm going to kill myself.' She reminds me of no one else and yet you feel you know her right away."

Joel also distinctively remembers introducing Julia to her *Flatliners* co-star, Kiefer Sutherland. "The minute they met, although they were quite shy with each other, there were definitely sparks."

Kiefer recalls, "I had no reason to like or dislike this person. There was no outside input except for my agent saying, 'Oh, I'm so glad Julia Roberts is doing this film.' And I was going, 'Julia who?' and thinking, 'OK, here's this novice.' Then she comes into rehearsal and she had a really incredible presence just as a person, which made me sit back and take a look. And then we started working together and I got really, really excited, because she was one of the best actors I'd ever worked with. I mean, she was incredibly giving, incredibly open and she had qualities that you can't even articulate when you're watching her work. And I thought that I had been the only one to see this and that I'd made this great find, until friends of mine who had seen screenings of *Steel Magnolias* said, 'Everybody knows that, Kiefer. Grow up.' "

One of the things that Sutherland was the most impressed with was the fact that she had the ability to instantly reflect the mood of whatever scene she was about to play in front of the camera. "She doesn't have to waste time with 'getting into the moment.' She can get there just like that."

Kiefer explained how his personal relationship with Julia developed. "We had been working together for over a month and our relationship really didn't take place for two months after that. So, I mean, my initial attraction to Julia was to her incredible talent as an actor. And I adopted a phenomenal, ridiculous respect that evolved into something else."

According to *Flatliners* director Joel Schumacher, "She has the kind of talent and the kind of screen presence where she can have a career for acting for as long as she wants to." One of the things that he found the most appealing was her ability to believ-

ably become so many different characters on
the screen. "There's this woman, this little
girl, this s**tkicker, this very innocent lady.
There's a *My Fair Lady* thing in there and I
think the reason she can pull it off is that all
those people are in her."

When *Flatliners* was released, it became a
big box-office hit. It was an imaginative
thriller of a film and it derived its jolts not
from murders or from monsters, but from
memories locked in the backs of people's
heads. The story centers on Rachel Mannus
(Julia Roberts) and her daredevil group of
friends in medical school. Having heard all
of the stories about people having afterlife
experiences only to return to the land of the
living, they are intrigued.

Nelson (Kiefer Sutherland) comes up with
the idea of being the first of the five of them
to have their hearts slowed to a complete
stop, their body temperatures lowered to 86
degrees Fahrenheit and then after a minute
or so, be brought back to life by electroshock.
He keeps repeating his morbid mantra,
"Today is a good day to die."

After being the first to be "flatlined,"
Nelson returns to life with tales of fantastic
images to report to his friends. He saw

enthralling images of soaring across the countryside. But there was something additional that he saw. It was a memory long repressed from his childhood. It involved tauntingly provoking a neighborhood boy until he fell to his death. Now Nelson must deal with the fact that he has unearthed the dead boy from his subconscious.

One by one the others bid for the honor and the thrill of flatlining next and they all have similar, haunting and very disturbing experiences. As Nelson so perfectly phrases it, "Somehow we brought our sins back physically and they're pissed."

As a thriller, *Flatliners* delivers a nice punch. Each of the four subjects who go on this experiment have adventures that are cinematically graphic and fascinating to watch. This makes for an effective and thought-provoking premise, because the ghosts of each individual exist only in their pasts and in their own heads. *Flatliners* became another hugely successful box-office hit for Julia. For a time period, it seemed that everything she touched turned to cinematic gold.

When the film was released in August 1980, the reviews were mixed. In *The Washington*

Post, Joe Brown's review amusingly pointed out, "Why did the medical student cross the line between life and death? To see what's on the other side. Sorry, but that's the basic premise of *Flatliners*, a Brat Pack neo-Gothic that plays like *Frankenstein* in reverse ... Julia Roberts signed to do *Flatliners* before she became a name and, though she's underused, she brings a serene restraint to her role."

In *The Chicago Sun-Times* Roger Ebert had problems with the pacing and complained, "Eventually the movie falls into a disappointing pattern, in which we're supposed to hold our breath while yet another voyager balances between life and death. One resuscitation is suspenseful. Two are fine. More than two wears out their welcomes." However, he found that the performances of the five leads ultimately made the film work. Wrote Ebert, "The cast, talented young actors, inhabit the shadows with the right mixture of intensity, fear and cockiness ... *Flatliners* is an original, intelligent thriller, well-directed by Joel Schumacher."

In addition to *Flatliners* becoming a box-office hit, it began Julia's relationship with Kiefer Sutherland. Julia herself explained, "He gives me a great sense of support. We're such great friends. If I come home ... and think my

day has been complete garbage, he's gonna
listen to that and not gonna say, 'You should be
happy.' I can have a lousy day. I don't have to be
grateful every second. He allows me the room
to do and feel and be everything."

Regarding her popularity, Julia claimed, "I
still find it rather scary—the crowds, the
premieres, the bodyguards. I worked with
people who have lost sight of their identities.
That isn't going to happen to me—I think."

When people suddenly become famous,
like Julia did in *Pretty Woman*, it affects
their lives differently. Some people are
stunned and frightened by it. They don't
know quite how it was thrust upon them and
they are petrified with fear at the prospect
that it could all disappear just as instanta-
neously as it had appeared. Other people let
it go to their heads. Instead of appreciating
it, they get a big head and start using their
power and influence in a negative way.

Julia Roberts was determined not to allow
herself to fall into either of these traps. She
was very confident in who she was and the
kind of person she was before she became
famous. "I'm flattered and I'm grateful," she
said in 1991, "but it's also not going to change
what I do. I don't reject it, but I don't whole-

heartedly incorporate it into my thoughts either. I don't walk around thinking, 'I light up the screen. OOH!' You still wake up in the morning and say, 'What am I supposed to do in this scene?' It's nice that people want to see my movies. My working all that time served a purpose. It obviously entertained people and that's why I do it."

CHAPTER FIVE

Making Choices

In the world of show business, a lot of people suddenly find themselves in the spotlight, heralded as new "stars." However, for most of them, the fame that they achieve is fleeting at best. The landscape is littered with "one hit wonders," especially in Hollywood. It is a long and difficult road to become a star, but even more challenging to try and maintain your success. In 1990, at the age of 22, Julia Roberts had arrived. Now, the question remained, "What is she going to do with it?" The pressure was on and the ball was in her court.

With the incredible popularity of *Pretty Woman* at the box office, there was nowhere she could go without being recognized. With regard to her public recognition factor, Julia recalls that suddenly "everything kind of tilted." Regarding the attention she was now receiving, she stated with amusement and dismay, "It's a very funny world we live in."

Joseph Ruben, her director in her next film, *Sleeping With the Enemy*, recalls, "This was a very emotional and topsy-turvy time for her. Strangers called her name, stopped her or even grabbed her on the street, while back at the hotel she'd get calls from fans who just wanted to chat."

On the journey of plotting her career, *Sleeping With the Enemy* was a great choice. When Julia elected to do the film, *Pretty Woman* had yet to catapult her to superstardom. However, by the time it was released, all eyes were on her. *Sleeping With the Enemy* seemed to be a perfect choice for her either way.

The film begins idyllically, opening with a scene of Julia Roberts as Sara, digging clams out of a sandy ocean shore. As her husband, Martin (Patrick Bergin) comes up to her, it seems that they are very much in love. However, it isn't long before we see that we are actually watching a woman on the verge of launching her great escape from a schizophrenic, sadistic maniac.

A major control freak with a psycho bent, the first time Martin is shown going over to the dark side is over a set of three hand towels, which aren't arranged with perfect symmetry. Next, we see Sara arranging the contents of the kitchen cupboard in perfect order just to please him.

When Martin goes off on a jealous rage, he blames Sara. To teach her a lesson, he hauls off and slaps her so hard she hits the floor, then he kicks her. Instead of dialing 911, Sara has a better plan. Martin insists that she take a nighttime sailboat ride with him, even though she has told him time and again that she is terrified of water and cannot swim.

As the boat hits stormy wind and waves, Sara drops off the side of the boat into the dark waters and swims to safety. While her husband and the rescue squad search for her body, she rushes back to the house, retrieves her prepacked survival kit of cash and clothes, and hits the road for parts unknown.

While filming *Sleeping With the Enemy*, Julia felt bolstered by frequent visits from the man whom she fondly referred to as "my boyfriend," Kiefer Sutherland. It seemed that she had at last found an emotional, supportive partner who was there for her and who knew about the stress and strain of long days on a movie set. For the time being, it seemed like the perfect relationship for her.

"I say to Julia, 'I'm really proud of how you've dealt with everything that's come your way,' " Kiefer claimed at the time. "There's a genuine quality to Julia that I don't think is taintable. She is ecstatic when things are going well and ecstatic when they're not going as well. That blows my mind. I envy it. It's something I aspire to and I'm in love with it till the cows come home."

There is one particular scene from the film *Sleeping With the Enemy*, where Patrick Bergin hits Julia, she falls to floor and he kicks her to stop her crying. Although she was actually laying on a piece of padding and there was a sandbag next to her leg for Bergin to kick, not everything always went as planned. During one take of the scene, she really hit the marble floor very hard with her head.

Although it was painful, Julia made it clear that she was willing to go to extraordinary means to get the perfect take, no matter how traumatic or harrowing it was. "I cracked the floor so hard that I had a black eye," she recounted. "And what made the take really that much more exciting was I cracked my head on the floor, I'm in so much pain and the actor that I was working with comes up to kick the sandbag, misses the sandbag and kicks me right in the leg. So I'm just a blithering idiot at this point. I cannot even see straight. When the take was over, the director said, 'I wanted to call, 'Cut,' and I said, 'If you'd have called 'Cut,' I would have wrung your neck. Cause I'm not gonna do that again.'"

It's all in a day's work according to Roberts: "It's gratifying to know that you did something that when people are gonna watch it, they're gonna go: 'Holy s**t, that looked like it hurt.' It better. Cause it did, you know! I really fell and my head bounced like a basketball on the marble floor and I can't tell you how much it hurt. I'm hysterical with pain. I'm crying. It's gone too far. And, Patrick comes to kick me and misses the sandbag and kicks me. It can't get any worse."

Recalls director Ruben, "I almost stopped the take. I thought she had hurt herself. Instead, what I did was open up this outpouring of tears and fear and emotion. She went all the way—to the point where everybody who was there was horrified. But she was willing to do that to get to that place where she needed to be."

In the scene where Julia has faked her own drowning, she rushes back to the house, knowing that her abusive husband will be occupied with the search party that is busy looking for her body in the dark. The house is cold and she has to play the whole scene in soaking wet underwear.

"It was absolutely freezing," recalls Roberts. "I said to the crew, 'I think we need a little group support here, so drop trousers. If you're not going to take your pants off, you can't stay in the house.' "

The lighting men stood there in their boxers or briefs. One mild-mannered and quiet cameraman startled everyone when he removed his pants to reveal a pair of fuchsia boxers with superhero comic action words on them like "Wham," "Zap" and "Bam."

Laughed Roberts, "It had nothing to do with acting and everything to do with just getting everybody as naked and cold as I was. And, I think everybody was very silently thrilled by it. It was the bonding thing, you know."

One of the things that Julia hated the most about the experiences of filming *Sleeping With the Enemy* were the weeks on location in

Abbeville and Spartanburg, South Carolina. According to her, "The people were horribly racist and I had a really hard time. I would go home and sit in the small room with my dog and say, 'So, there's nothing to eat ... you wanna go to sleep?' I didn't feel like I was on location anymore. I didn't feel like I had a job. I felt like this hell was where I lived."

With all of the growth and change Julia had experienced in her own life, she found that when she visited the Deep South—a geographic area she once called "home"—there seemed to be absolutely no change and little tolerance for forward-thinking liberal mentality. "I go back and see that there's been no movement in time. I am so easily enraged by the flailing ignorance, which is tossed about as if it's God's words. In Abbeville I felt so assaulted and insulted by these people that I just didn't care to be nice anymore."

She went to one restaurant and was deeply offended by the way black people were treated there. "I told the owner, 'You shouldn't call this place Michael's, you should call it Bigot's!'" she claims.

When *Sleeping With the Enemy* was released in February 1991, the reviews were decidedly mixed. Peter Travers, one of Julia

Roberts' strongest champions in the press,
claimed, "Julia Roberts, a beauty who can
also act, is one of the best things in recent
movies. By my count she hasn't made a really
good movie yet ... But don't get your hopes up
about *Sleeping With the Enemy* ... Though
Sleeping rouses itself for a corker of a climax,
by then it has lost its claim to be anything
more than a serviceable shocker. Roberts
remains a marvel. But she still hasn't found
the movie to test her talents."

Roger Ebert in *The Chicago Sun-Times*
was disappointed with *Sleeping With the
Enemy*. He claimed, "I found myself watching the film in sinking spirits. The opening
scenes on the beach were effective and held
my attention. Then the middle passages of
the movie, where Bergin discovers the
deception and goes looking for Roberts,
began to disillusion me ... *Sleeping With the
Enemy* is a movie that briefly seems to have
greatness in its grasp and goes straight for
the mundane."

According to Rita Kempley in *The
Washington Post*, "*Sleeping With the Enemy*
is merely *Fatal Attraction* with a splash of
Brut—a relentlessly formulated look at the
downside of sexual obsession ... Julia Roberts

is lush but never allowed to be lustrous
as Laura, a tentative beauty who is fiendishly
abused by her financier husband ...
Ultimately, *Sleeping With the Enemy* wants
to be about one woman's rebirth, but Roberts
neither grows nor glows in this empty movie
... She's *Pretty Woman* with a gun."

Regardless of what any of the critics said,
Sleeping With the Enemy was a hit at the box
office. Taking a look at the bottomline
figures of how much money her films were
producing at the time proved this point brilliantly. In 1988, *Satisfaction* had grossed
$7.8 million dollars. *Mystic Pizza*, also
released in 1988, took in a respectable $12.8
million. Her ensemble hit, *Steel Magnolias*,
grossed an impressive $79.4 million at the
box office when it was released in 1989. And,
the biggest hit of all, *Pretty Woman*, which
came out in 1990 had hit a whopping $178.4
million. On its heels, *Sleeping With the
Enemy* raked in a very outstanding $97.7
million. There was simply something about
Julia Roberts that instantly spelled "success."

Perhaps part of it was that her skittishness
transferred brilliantly on the screen. More often
than not, this essence was described in the
press as her "coltish" quality. She laughed, "What

is this association with me and horses? It's the season for me to be 'coltish!' But, what a great word. I mean, I love horses. So it's a wonderful word, a wonderful association. I wholeheartedly accept it. I mean, I've been called a lot worse, so I'm kinda digging 'coltish.'"

After *Sleeping With the Enemy*, she was starting to feel a little frazzled around the edges. According to Julia in 1990, "It's funny, because I've spent the last year and a half making movies and giving and giving and giving. There would be nothing left and I'd find one more thing, so I'd give that. But there comes a point where you're losing sleep and it takes a long time to get anything back from all that giving. It's a great thing to have the opportunity to give like that—but at the same time, you know, when you have family, friends and there's love in your life, and you give to that, you can see instant gratification. You can see somebody smile or just pick somebody up or something. And it's easier to give that way than it is to just be giving to this ... black machinery."

By 1991, when talk about her private life began to collide with her career, Julia started to become a bit defensive. "My relationships happened over three years of my life, not some wild, outrageous weekend. I think what keeps me from getting really annoyed is the security I feel in what I know. Yes, movies sometimes promote a fantasy that can be confusing, but that also comes from someone whose life is already confused. And I've been in that situation. But at this point, my life is very clear."

Julia was weighing out her priorities. "I mean, acting is the true love of mine, but it's not the true love. There are times when I get so bogged down by the politics of this business that I just have these great domestic fantasies. Being at home, and being quiet, and reading, and having a garden and doing all that stuff. Taking care of a family. Those are the most important things. Movies will come and go, but family is a real kind of rich consistency."

While Julia had never been married, Kiefer had. He had an ex-wife, Camila Kath, and together they had a daughter before divorcing.

Kiefer's mother, actress Shirley Douglas, found Julia delightful. "The movie business is a small cocoon and the fear of failure is massive. They help each other not to take things too seriously," she said of Julia and Kiefer's relationship. "At Julia's age—really, at any age—it's remarkable to see someone not dithering."

As Julia herself stated at the time, "We're just real happy. I've been lucky to find somebody who I not only like and is my best friend, but who I so admire and respect and have fallen madly in love with. I've been immensely blessed in the discovery of this person."

Very much in love with each other, they decided to get married. They did their best to keep their schedules aligned so that they could spend as much time with each other as possible once engaged. "When you're on a shoot for three months," claimed Julia, "you change and even you don't know how. That's too much to ask of somebody, to come back and say, 'I'm really different, figure it out.' This decision puts another twist in the finagling of getting a job, but in the end, I would assume, it's a hell of a lot easier than coming home to a stranger and saying, 'Where the hell have you been and who are you?' "

One of the privileges of sudden stardom was the fact that Julia's living situation drastically changed for the better. She was finally able to move from her tiny apartment into a million-dollar Hollywood Hills house.

"There were books and papers scattered all over my apartment," she said. "The house needed a paint job and it was just too much.

I had so much in storage that my girlfriends and I joked about a whole town called Storage, California. You know, 'Where's your stuff?' 'In Storage.' But while I was gone, Kiefer took care of the whole thing. I came home to find the house all ready, even my clothes hanging in the closet. Astonishing!"

There was, however, talk of Julia continuing her flirtatious ways, even though she was engaged to Kiefer. In September 1995, it was reported that Julia and John F. Kennedy Jr. spent two days together in 1990, when Kennedy was going with Daryl Hannah and while Roberts was engaged to Sutherland. Their fling supposedly took place in the Four Seasons Hotel in Los Angeles, where John Jr. was staying, however after those two days, Julia flew back to New York City and that was the end of it.

Regardless of the validity of the JFK Jr. claim, there was trouble in paradise in the Roberts/Sutherland camp. For whatever reason, just as quickly as Julia had fallen in love with Kiefer, she seemed to fall out of love with him. From the outside, it appeared that they were madly in love and perfect for each other. They set a wedding date for Friday, June 14, 1991. It was scheduled to be an elaborate

Hollywood affair, staged more like a scene from a movie than a private couple's wedding. In fact, it was to be held on massive Soundstage 14 on the 20th Century Fox lot decorated like a garden with trellises and a real sod lawn.

Julia's gown was a custom-tailored two-piece dress with a long jacket. The long skirt and the train could be broken away to reveal a minidress underneath and cost in the neighborhood of $8,000. There were to be four bridesmaids, including actress Deborah Porter, makeup artist Lucienne Zammit and Julia's talent agents Elaine Goldsmith and Risa Shapiro. The quartet of would-be bridesmaids had already picked up their $425 Manolo Blahnik shoes, which had been the exact green of the dresses they were to wear.

The cake was to be a four-tier confectionary creation decorated with sugared violets and green icing ribbons. Dominick's restaurant, which was to host Kiefer's bachelor party, had already baked a "grooms cake" for that event.

Suddenly, just four days before the wedding, Julia called it off. "Believe me, it was humiliating," she explained. "I was shopping for bridesmaids' bouquets when it struck me that everything wasn't right. I'm still very upset, but I'm proud of myself for not being a doormat. I've learned you absolutely can sustain life without sex."

Kiefer was reportedly very hurt by this sudden move. In retaliation, he reportedly went to the press and told them that sex with Julia was like having "a corpse" in bed.

Following the row, Julia suddenly dropped out of a film that she was going to be in with Sutherland. They had been planning to co-star in a Western called *Renegades*. She explained, "I don't have to do anything I don't want to. Your life is as pressure-filled as you allow it to be. Sometimes I feel people try to make it more difficult, to see how absolutely taxing they can make your life."

Apparently, there were several aspects to Julia and Kiefer's relationship woes. One of the problems was the fact that Julia was to be paid more than Kiefer for *Renegades*. She was set to receive the overwhelming fee of $7.5 million, while her co-star and fiancé was to be taking home $2.5 million. Her salary was double the price that he was used to commanding for his acting talents.

Another problem had to do with Kiefer's relationship with 24-year-old go-go dancer Amanda Rice. Amanda worked in the Crazy

Girls Club in Hollywood under the stage name
of "Raven." In February 1991, Kiefer moved out
of Julia's house and took a $105-a-week room
at a seedy Hollywood hotel, the St. Francis,
which was so bare and bargain-rate it did not
even have a private phone in it. Reportedly,
renting the room was part of his research for a
film called *In From the Cold*, which Kiefer ultimately did not end up doing. However, during
his stay at The St. Francis Hotel, he hung out
with Amanda at a local pool hall called
Hollywood Billiards Parlor. The press had a
field day when the two of them were spotted at
Disneyland on a day trip with Kiefer's 3-year-
old daughter Sarah and Amanda's young son.

After moving back in with Julia, Kiefer
continued to visit Amanda at the billiard parlor. He would come in around closing time
and they would be seen leaving together.

Kiefer's personal publicist, Annett Wolf,
explained: "He has never denied that he met
her, because he likes to play pool. He's deny-
ing that he had a relationship with her. He is
extremely upset about this thing with Rice.
There was nothing sexual."

On June 9, 1991, during a break in her
busy filming schedule, and just days before
her scheduled wedding to Kiefer, Julia

Roberts went to Tucson, Arizona, to relax at the world-famous Canyon Ranch health and beauty spa. While there, she ran into actor Jason Patric.

Witnesses in the dining room of Canyon Ranch saw Julia and Jason sharing at least one meal together. And when they left, it looked like he was consoling her.

The very next day she flew back to Los Angeles and called off her wedding.

June 14, 1991 was supposed to be the day that Roberts and Sutherland were married. Instead, he packed his things and moved out of her house. While he was vacating her place, she was seen with Jason Patric again, munching on a turkey burger at the "in" eatery, The Nowhere Cafe. Only hours after that luncheon date, the two of them boarded a plane for London. From London they flew up to Dublin, Ireland, and took two rooms at the Shelbourne Hotel. The engagement ring was off her finger and press photographers hounded the hotel, trying to get a photo of the new couple together.

The breakup of Julia Roberts and Kiefer Sutherland was the hot bit of gossip of the summer. According to entertainment columnist Liz Smith, the affair with Kiefer "caused her a lot of trouble. I think the luck-iest thing that ever happened to her was to cancel her marriage, although she was totally discombobulated by it. But I don't think it's calming when you're rushing from one love affair to the next. I think it would be great if she concentrated on her career and not the men in her life."

While all of the drama over her wedding cancellation was going on, she had yet another movie in the theaters. Her summer 1991 film release, *Dying Young,* had just come out on June 21 and was being met with highly mixed results.

Dying Young director Joel Schumacher loved working with Julia again. She was just as charming as he had remembered when they collaborated on *Flatliners*. He especially liked her versatility and her ability to convinc-ingly become the characters she portrayed on the screen. "I don't think there's anyone like Julia," he claimed. "She's a true original. She can be the sexiest and the shyest, the most ladylike, the most vulnerable and the most street-smart."

Julia's co-star in the film was actor Campbell Scott, who was very impressed by her ability to handle her newfound fame with both grace and agility. "I think she's handling this whole thing unbelievably well," he said. "As an actress she has beautiful presence, people find her identifiable and accessible."

As *Dying Young* opens, Hilary (Julia Roberts) makes the discovery that her boyfriend is sleeping with another woman. She moves out on him immediately and back in with her totally ditzy mother, (Ellen Burstyn).

Hilary soon applies for a job to be a care-giver at a wealthy Nob Hill house.

The position was to be the personal nurse/companion for the son of a rich busi-nessman named Victor (Campbell Scott). Victor has cancer and in addition to needing assistance, he is also seeking a reason to go on living. In Hilary, he finds both. Naturally, her charge falls in love with her.

The critics seemed to unanimously dislike the film altogether. In the *Salt Lake City Deseret News*, Chris Hicks wrote, "*Dying Young* is sort of *Love Story* by way of *Pretty Woman* ... The result is a soft, sentimental, somewhat sappy romance that loses its edge quickly and becomes a by-the-numbers Hollywood fantasy ... This isn't a bad movie, really. It's just one we've seen too many times before, mostly on television. The only difference here is Julia Roberts in the lead role—not to mention an abundance of four-letter words."

And Joe Brown in *The Washington Post* found *Dying Young* to be a film that had been told many times, with stronger results: "The summer bummer *Dying Young* has been baited with current hot-property Julia Roberts ... Roberts plays a spunky, beautiful working girl who hires herself out to a wealthy, good-looking young man. Only this time she's emotionally for hire ... It's hard to sit through *Dying Young* without sensing a thematic undercurrent about AIDS. Perhaps *Dying Young* can be seen as a way of stirring sympathy in the mainstream moviegoing audiences who stayed away in droves from *Longtime Companion,* a superior film on a similar subject."

After *Dying Young,* Julia needed a movie that was much lighter in subject matter. When the offer came around for her to be one of the stars of Steven Spielberg's big budget retelling of *Peter Pan,* playing Tinkerbell in *Hook,* it seemed like the perfect change of pace for her.

Speaking of her role as the sprightly fairy Tinkerbell, Julia explained, "She's kind of an updated Tinkerbell. I don't think she's the one that everyone grew up with. She's very clever and funny. She has kind of a bite to her."

A big-screen adaptation of the children's classic story *Peter Pan*, *Hook* had problems from the start. Taking an enchanting story like the one of Neverland and its inhabitants, making it relevant to jaded 1990s audiences, modernizing the characters and toying with the script in a heavy-handed direction had built-in pitfalls.

The idea behind this updated fairy tale relies on several stretches of the imagination—in Neverland logic—to set up several anachronistic plot twists. Here's the premise: Wendy Darling left Neverland in the early part of the 1900s, leaving Peter Pan to remain ageless in Neverland. However, on one of his visits to the real world, he fell in love with Wendy's granddaughter. He made the decision to grow up and grow old with her. However, in the process, he somehow forgot all about Captain Hook, the Lost Boys and his whole past.

Modern day Peter (Robin Williams) is a cell-phone-carrying stressed-out workaholic. He takes his family to London to meet the real Wendy (Maggie Smith) and to see her honored with the dedication of the wing of a children's hospital named for her.

When Peter's children are kidnapped by Captain Hook (Dustin Hoffman), he is forced to go back to Neverland to rescue to him. Enter Julia Roberts as the fairy with attitude: Tinkerbell.

After a disastrous confrontation between Peter and Captain Hook and his cartoon-like pirates, Tinkerbell has three days to re-teach Peter to fly so he will be ready to battle Captain Hook for the lives of his children. As delightful as the prospect of Julia Roberts as Tinkerbell seems, she really isn't given the chance to shine. There is a sequence where she uses her magic powers and grows to life-size to make a romantic play for Peter Pan. However, there seems to be zero sparkle in the Tinkerbell/Peter Pan pairing. Her performance seemed joyless. Perhaps part of the problem was that she filmed *Hook* at the same time she was breaking up with Kiefer Sutherland. Her unhappiness seemed to show on Tinkerbell's face.

When it opened in December 1991, the reviews for *Hook* were mainly awful. Just like *Dying Young* before it, the critics hated it. *TV Guide* claimed, "*Hook*'s problems begin with its screenplay, a clumsy attempt to meld reality and fantasy which leaves too many issues unresolved ... As top-heavy as Captain Hook's ornate, immobile ship, this lavish, elaborate production ultimately collapses under its own weight."

Reviewing for BBC1 in England, Almar Haflidason dismissed *Hook* by stating, "Steven Spielberg's updating of the story of Peter Pan is a messy and incoherent effort but there are nevertheless many enjoyable moments in this noisy and vigorous affair. There's certainly no criticizing the splendid sets and costume designs."

It seemed that Hal Hinson in *The Washington Post* was the only critic who enjoyed *Hook*. According to him, "It's also great fun: big, splashy, energetic, one-size-fits-all Hollywood entertainment. Spielberg and Co. have finally made their Disney movie—or better yet, their film version of a theme park at Disneyland. It's sort of like Pirates of the Caribbean and It's a Small World rolled into one. It's a helluva contraption and certainly one to be marveled at. It gives good ride."

A perfect Christmas season film, *Hook* took in nearly $300 million worldwide. Since it was the kind of film that a family could go and see, and since children don't read reviews, it actually did well at the box office. And, although it was a bit heavy-handed in the direction, it had some visually stunning elements that were undeniable. In January 1992, *Hook* was nominated for five Academy Awards, including Best Art Direction, Best Visual Effects, Best Makeup, Best Song for *When You're Alone* and Best Costume Design.

After the disappointing box-office non-successes of *Dying Young* and *Hook*, Julia did something very revolutionary: She took nearly two years off from the screen. Her *Dying Young* director, Joel Schumacher claimed, "I think it was one of the smartest, healthiest, most self-protective moves she could have made. She had made so many movies and had instant success thrust upon her—with its insanity and pressure—at such a young age. Julia is very, very smart and I think all of her smarts were telling her it was time to be self-protective."

Peter Bart, an editor of show business magazine *Variety*, agreed. "I think the year off was smart. She was risking overexposure. And most important of all, she needed it. The most important thing is to keep your own identity in place and she was going over the edge."

The one and only appearance that Julia

Roberts made on the big screen during her hiatus came in a brief, less-than-five-minutes cameo role in the all-star Robert Altman satire, *The Player*. It was a perfect choice for her.

The Player is all about the world that exists within the movie business in Hollywood. After being immersed in that world for a period of time, people confuse fantasy for reality. At the beginning of the film, we see movie studio executive Griffin Mill being pitched on movie story ideas by everyone he comes in contact with.

Meanwhile, someone is also sending Griffin threatening notes. Assuming that he knows who the threatening screenplay writer is, Griffin seeks him out in a cinema in Pasadena. The writer, David Kahane (Vincent D'Onofrio), picks an argument with Griffin and he is accidentally killed in a parking lot scuffle.

Already paranoid about someone following him, when the threatening notes keep on arriving, he knows he has killed an innocent man. One of the films that is being pitched to Griffin by Tom Okley (Richard E. Grant) and Andy Civella (Dean Stockwell) involves a woman facing her own execution in the gas chamber at San Quentin.

At the end of the film, we get to see the

finished product of the story. Screening the last minutes of the film, we see that it stars Julia Roberts as the doomed woman. Awaiting the execution are reporters played by Susan Sarandon and Peter Falk. Julia is seen being given Last Rites and then she is marched into the gas chamber. The gas permeates the chamber and at the last second her reprieve phone call comes in. Bruce Willis shoots out the glass windows of the gas chamber and rescues her. As she is being whisked away from the arms of death by Willis, Julia says her only line, "What took you so long?"

A totally entertaining film from beginning to end, *The Player* was a prestigious showcase for Julia to let her fans know that she was still alive and well, in spite of her two-year sabbatical.

Recalls director Robert Altman, "To play themselves in *The Player*, I called everybody I knew. There were a lot of celebrities that graciously gave their time and came out." According to Altman, he very much got the joke about the movie as he was making it. "I was making fun of myself and people who make films," he admits.

The Player was the surprise box-office hit of 1992. According to Hal Hinson of *The*

Washington Post, "Altman loves practical jokes, and *The Player* is his craftiest prank, his jolly last laugh." Deeson Howe raved, "*The Player* is a rare commodity. It's brilliant and a guilty pleasure." Peter Travers of *Rolling Stone* concurred, saying: "[Altman] sticks it to every target, himself and us included, with a wicked zest that hurts only when you laugh."

And Neil Smith of BBC1 claimed, "It's a masterly distillation of Tinseltown foibles which also works as a compelling moral thriller and a commentary on the cult of celebrity."

In 1993, after enjoying her hiatus, Julia finally had to start considering what would be the project that would return her to a starring role on the big screen. According to her, "I was determined not to compromise, not to go back to work just because I was afraid people might stop calling. I thought, 'Damn it, if it takes five years, I'm going to wait for a script that I really want to do.' It was a good exercise in not trying to keep momentum just for momentum's sake."

Dying Young and *Hook* had been major mistakes for her and she knew it. Now it was time to jump-start her career. Appearing briefly at the end of *The Player* was an inspired move for Julia. She was wonderful in her tongue-in-cheek role in the satirical film. It was just enough to remind theater audiences of her magnetism on camera and it made audiences long for much more of her. She would make it worth the wait!

CHAPTER SIX

Give Them Something To Talk About

$\mathcal{I}$n 1992, both Julia Roberts and Lyle Lovett had been seen in Robert Altman's *The Player*. However, none of their scenes was together. It was while she was in New Orleans in May 1993, filming what was to be known as her "comeback" movie—

The Pelican Brief—that their paths crossed again. According to Lyle Lovett, the chemistry between them suddenly clicked: "It felt extraordinary. It just felt right. But I didn't want to actually think it out loud, or even to myself, because of her being who she is. I knew I really liked this person. But I thought: 'Don't be stupid. She's Julia Roberts.'"

The couple went through a whirlwind month-long courtship and on June 27, Julia married Lyle at a small Lutheran church in Marion, Indiana. She was literally a barefoot bride at the ceremony. That night, Lyle had a concert performance in Noblesville, Indiana, and Julia joined him on stage to sing a duet version of the Tammy Wynette classic, *Stand By Your Man*, in front of an audience of 10,000 people.

No one was more surprised than Lyle, who admitted, "I supposed it is intriguing that she'd marry me. I bet a lot of people might think that makes her one of the 25 Most Stupid People of the Year."

In the fall 1993, Lyle claimed of Julia's cooking, "I've liked everything." And, of the marriage: "We've never gone more than a week without seeing each other since we got married. But before that we'd never spent more than seven days together. We're just so happy to be together when we can be."

Julia claimed of their marriage, "I feel liberated in a way. I feel like this really pleasant calm has descended upon my life. It has to do with your own ability to make a perfectly correct decision. I think that's quite a feat, to look at something you've done and say, 'This is completely right.' Every time I talk to him ... or look at his picture ... or think about him, I think, 'Wow, I'm so ... I'm so smart, I'm so lucky.' He makes me so happy, he's so good to me.

"We are pretending to be a normal couple. We get up in the morning, we have breakfast, he goes off to work, I go off to work, we come home at night. 'How was your day, dear?' That whole gig."

A friend of Julia's who was at the wedding said, "I don't know if we actually heard her say she 'loved' Lyle. We just reckoned she had to because of the way she kept smiling. It was a very smiley wedding, a very happy occasion, but somehow unreal because it had all happened so fast."

Now that her personal life seemed to finally be in order, it was time to focus on her career. Julia had now experienced being a big box-office hit and she had also been on the

downside as well. According to her, "It
certainly doesn't hurt when you pack 'em into
the theater. But at the same time, you can't do
anything to get people to go to the movie."
Well, it was time to find a movie that would
get her fans AND the general public into the
movie theaters to see her again. The exciting
John Grisham project known as *The Pelican
Brief* seemed like just the right project for her.

Having had several of his novels such as
The Firm and *The Client* made into highly
successful movies, in the early 1990s writer
John Grisham had full intentions of seeing
his latest project, a book called *The Pelican
Brief*, made into a film as well. In fact, he
sold the rights to director and producer Alan
J. Pakula before it was even written.

According to Grisham, he actually had Julia
Roberts in mind when he wrote *The Pelican
Brief* and he thought that she would be
perfect for the role of ambitious and clever
Darby. When the novel was finished, Julia
read it, liked it and agreed to star in the film.
This was all prior to her even seeing the script.

The film was shot on location in
Washington, D.C., New Orleans and New
York. The costumes worn in the film were
specifically chosen to bring to life the many

moods of the story, as well as the subtle but purposeful use of color. At the beginning of the film, when Darby is with her professor/lover, Callahan (Sam Shepard), the colors surrounding their scenes are very warm and light. This was to psychologically depict her world with him as safe and warm. Also, the character of Darby wore many wigs throughout to disguise her as she ran from potential assassins. According to the film's costume designer, Albert Wolsky, "We found a way to try to make her as invisible as possible, using no color in her clothes, only beiges and taupes, to blend [in with the surrounding scenery.]"

The settings in which she hid, were carefully chosen as well. Explains production designer Philip Rosenberg: "Alan wanted all of the hotel rooms to be very drab and anonymous. So we created a palette of wallpapers, drained of colors, mostly mauves, none of them memorable."

In the film, a hit man has been hired to end Supreme Court Justice Rosenberg's long career (Hume Cronyn) and to murder Supreme Court Justice Jenson (Ralph Cosham) as well. This will leave two vacancies for the current President of the United

States to fill their posts with men who politically think the way that he does.

Thomas Callahan is a law professor at Tulane University in New Orleans. Darby Shaw, age 24, is not only one of his star students, she is also his girlfriend. When Thomas and Darby discuss the deaths of the two Supreme Court Justices, she decides to come up with a theory of what the motive may have been for the two murders—which were obviously linked.

Similarly, newspaper reporter Gray Grantham (Denzel Washington) is trying to solve the same murderous puzzle. When Darby comes up with her intriguingly plausible theory on the case, she calls it *The Pelican Brief.* When Callahan passes a copy of the theory to one of his friends in Washington, D.C., who works at the White House, things start to happen with a domino effect. It seems that her theory is right on target and people start turning up dead in an effort to keep *The Pelican Brief* under wraps.

This movie is filled with desperate people resorting to desperate measures. Along the way, there are some great performances, including Robert Culp as the baffled President of the United States, John

Lithgow as Grantham's exasperated editor and Stanley Tucci as a calculating hit man.

There is one exciting chase scene after another in this excellently paced and fast-moving film. After her two-year vacation from the screen, Julia Roberts is at her vulnerable but tough-as-nails best. Also, she and Denzel Washington work very well together, as both are actors who can shift gears between "rational" and "emotional" with believable ease. *The Pelican Brief* is fast-paced, suspenseful and totally entertaining.

When the film was released in December 1993, critics either loved it or hated it. In *The Chicago Sun-Times*, Roger Ebert wrote of *The Pelican Brief*, "Because the atmosphere is skillfully drawn, because the actors are well cast and because Pakula knows how to construct a sequence to make it work, the movie delivers while it's onscreen ... One thing the movie proves conclusively is the value of star power. Julia Roberts, returning after two years off the screen, makes a wonderful heroine—warm, courageous, very beautiful. Denzel Washington shows again how credible he seems on the screen; like Spencer Tracy, he can make you believe in almost any character. Together they have a real chemistry."

But Chris Hicks of *Salt Lake City Deseret News* complained, "Too many characters, too much plotting and not enough suspense to keep it all moving." Likewise, Marc Savlov of the *Austin Chronicle* in Austin, Texas, found, "*The Pelican Brief* comes across as a pro-longed bout with deja vu: You know you've seen this before and more than once at that ... Grisham's novel was no landmark of literary originality to begin with, but Pakula stream-lines the story into a corner and then lets it run 30 minutes longer than necessary." And Shannon J. Harvery of *The Sunday Times* in Australia called *The Pelican Brief* an "utterly confusing John Grisham story, with Roberts and Washington in full stereotype mode."

Critics aside, the moviegoing public made *The Pelican Brief* Julia's next box-office hit. As much as her life seemed to be a Cinderella story, she also experienced some of the less-than-glamorous aspects of the life of a superstar. During 1993, she was plagued by one of her first stalkers.

There was one particular fan who was sending threatening letters. At first, the person's intentions didn't seem all that alarming. However, in time, the nature of the letters shifted from fan-like to obsessive to sexual and, finally, to threatening. Enough so that while filming portions of *The Pelican Brief*, Julia was surrounded by bodyguards at all times. There was also a planned secrecy to her whereabouts at all times.

On a break from filming in New Orleans, Julia had something of a scare. She announced that she was going to go off on her own to buy a cup of espresso coffee. However, she was mobbed by a group of eager fans and she panicked. Hailing a police officer, she was able to smoothly escape, but the incident freaked her out. It gave her a glimpse at how accessible she could be in public. Furthermore, the character that she played in *The Pelican Brief* was one who was being stalked by killers.

Unfortunately, the stalker incident caused Julia to be very aware of her security at all times. From that point onward, she simply had to get used to having bodyguards present whenever she wandered off of the protective environment of the film set.

It did not, however, deter her from her career. Julia's next project was *Ready to Wear*, another film directed by Robert Altman. Lyle Lovett had a part in the film as well.

Ready to Wear (also known as its French

title *Prêt-à-Porter*) promised to be the perfect sequel to *The Player* and its release was
much heralded. However, it received many
mixed reviews and didn't do all that well at
the box office. Yet, for many movie buffs, it
was a tongue-in-cheek favorite.

Ready to Wear is filled with inside humor
about Paris—more specifically, about the
completely lunatic fashion business. Anorexic
models, flamboyant queens dressing as
women and the pretentiousness of it all each
get skewered in this razor-sharp satire.

In the film, real fashion designers—such as
Christian Lacroix, Terry Mugler, Jean-Paul
Gaultier—play their outrageous selves.
Likewise, some of the most famous models
in the business—including Claudia Schiffer,
Naomi Campbell and Linda Evangelista—
are seen on the runways, strutting their stuff.

Julia Roberts, a member of the fashion
press, is a reporter from Houston named
Anne Eisenhower. She has lost her suitcase
and is stuck in her only outfit, a stained
T-shirt. When she arrives at her hotel, there
is a room shortage and she finds herself
doing battle with another reporter, Joe
Flynn (Tim Robbins), for the rights to the
same room. Like playing "King of the Castle,"

they both rush into the same room—which seems to be the last available one in Paris that week—and they square off for territory.

Then there are the stars showing up as themselves just to see the show—including Cher and Harry Belafonte. There is also a mysterious couple of married buyers from Marshall Fields department store (Danny Aiello and Teri Garr). It seems that he not only likes to purchase lines of women's clothing for his store chain, but he also likes dressing up in drag.

Although this is the second Robert Altman film that featured both Julia Roberts and Lyle Lovett as stars, they never have a single scene together. All of Lyle's scenes are with Lauren Bacall and all of Julia's are with Tim Robbins.

There's plenty of double dealing, backstabbing and sex going on amidst all of the sumptuous and sometimes ridiculous fashion and audiences either loved it or hated it. When the film was released in the theaters on Christmas day 1994, several publications concurred. *Playboy* magazine gave it four stars and called it "Good fun!" *The Seattle Times* raved that it was "Sexy and hilarious!" In *Tucson Weekly*, Zachary Woodruff wrote, "Authentic Parisian settings, interviews with real designers and the commemorative inclusion of Italian actors Marcello Mastroianni, Anouk Aimee and Sophia Loren can't save the movie from its aimless one-joke premise ... Julia Roberts fans will want to note, however, that Altman extracts what is easily Roberts' finest performance in a sub-plot that pits her against Tim Robbins for a spark-filled weekend romance in a hotel room."

According to Roger Ebert of *The Chicago Sun-Times*, "The fashion industry is the most sublimely silly of human enterprises, making billions by convincing most of the human race to dress interchangeably and the rest to dress like the victims of a cruel jest ... There are some nice moments here. Robbins and Roberts, who hardly leave their room, create the bittersweet sense of a self-contained affair that has no reference to their real lives ... There is also an undeniable pleasure simply in people-watching ... The result is a little like a comedy crossed with a home movie."

Although everyone was talking about Julia's success and ability as an actress, her not-as-public personal life had its problems. While she was filming her next movie, *I Love Trouble*, certain facts about her relationship with her older brother, Eric, came to light. In the early '90s, he had broken up with his longtime girlfriend, Kelly Cunningham. Together they had a daughter, Emma, who was 3 years old at the time that *I Love Trouble* was filmed in 1994. According to an "insider" on the set, 27-year-old Aunt Julia received a call one day from Kelly asking her if she could watch her niece, little Emma.

The insider explained, "When Kelly asked her if she could keep an eye on Emma for the day, Julia told her: 'I'd love to watch her as long as you don't mind her hanging out with me on the set.' Kelly agreed that would be OK. When Kelly dropped Emma off on the set, Julia immediately ran up to her and gave her a big hug. Emma had a big smile on her face and looked excited. Julia looked like she was really enjoying herself. It made a nice change for her—Julia sometimes looks a bit bored or unhappy when she's working."

The on-set source revealed, "Julia is crazy about Emma. When she wasn't hugging and kissing her, the two chatted and giggled. It's obvious Julia will make a terrific mom. She watched over Emma like a hawk. Whenever Julia came out of her trailer, she'd always have Emma with her. When Julia went to get her hair and makeup done, so did Emma."

Julia's charming day with her niece Emma

only fueled reports about the bitter feud between her and Emma's father, Eric. It seemed that when Eric and Kelly split up, he launched a strong legal battle to have Kelly declared an unfit mother, so that he could have sole custody of Emma. Knowing of Eric's use of cocaine, his faltering career choices and his less-than-stable life, Julia sided with Kelly—feeling that Emma should be with her mother and not erratic Eric. In fact, Julia was so insistent that her brother be defeated in his custody battle, that she personally spent a reported thousands of dollars hiring a top-notch lawyer to represent Kelly.

To further sever her relationship with her brother, Julia stopped talking to him in 1991. It is a rift in their relationship that has never been repaired. "I was a big help to Julia when she started out, so it's hurtful to see her behave so coldly now," said Eric. "I broke up with Kelly for valid reasons and I didn't want to make my child miserable by trying to spend the rest of my life with this woman."

Julia's relationship with her own husband was not doing much better. June 27, 1994 was Julia and Lyle's first wedding anniversary, but they were more than 5,000 miles apart at the time. Julia was in the British

Isles filming *Mary Reilly* and Lyle was in
Los Angeles, working on a video for his
latest album, *I Love Everybody*.

According to a friend of Lyle's: "He worked
right through their anniversary. When I
asked him about it, he said, 'Anniversary? I
don't expect we'll do anything. Julia is in
London and I've got my work here in Los
Angeles.'" It clearly seemed that the spark of
their romance had all but died.

That same week in June came Julia's next
film release. In it, she teamed up with Nick
Nolte in the comedy/drama *I Love Trouble*. At
the time, it seemed to be an ideal choice for
Julia. It had enough dramatic suspense scenes
to make it a bit of a mystery and enough comedy elements to show off her cinematic charms.

In *I Love Trouble*, Julia and Nick play
reporters on two rival Windy City newspapers. Nolte is Peter Brackett, a famous columnist for the *The Chicago Chronicle*, who gets
by on his charisma and his charm, as much as
for his writing talent. Roberts is Sabrina
Peterson, an eager new hotshot investigative
reporter on *The Chicago Globe*.

There are some great character actors who
show up throughout the film, especially
Olympia Dukakis as his sharp-tongued

secretary and *Saturday Night Live*'s Nora Dunn as his literary publicist. Robert Loggia is great as his no-nonsense newspaper editor and Marsha Mason as a cool and elegant Senator Gayle Robbins. Comedian Eugene Levy is also appropriately goofy as a Las Vegas wedding chapel justice of the peace.

When a train derails, Brackett is pressured into covering the story for his newspaper. There stands Sabrina Peterson, asking all of the right questions at a press briefing following the wreck. When she announces to Brackett that he may as well hold his breath if he thinks he is going to get to first base with her sexually, he snaps back at her, "Where did you say you're from? Bitchville?"

Newspaper novice Sabrina ends up scooping Brackett on her very first front-page headlined story. With that, the escalating rivalry between the pair has them off and running as they launch into an attempt to outdo each other.

Naturally, along the way, Sabrina and Peter's rivalry turns from professional competition to romance, but not before they both escape from a murder attempt and an assassin provoked carjacking. Throughout the film, Julia is a charming spitfire and Nolte makes a great suave scoundrel.

Despite Roberts and Nolte's performances, *I Love Trouble* failed to capture a strong box-office audience. Defending the film, Julia claimed, "Quite frankly, I can watch the movie. I saw a screening of the movie. There were things about it that were funny. I didn't walk out of there saying, 'What a hideous disaster! What was I thinking?' Where I feel disappointment is that the original concept of the movie sort of trickled away."

When it was released in June 1994, it wasn't strongly received by the press. Rita Kempley in *The Washington Post* wrote, "*I Love Trouble*, a facile caper about rival newspaper reporters, is a lot like an IKEA bookcase: It's easily assembled and stylishly utilitarian ... Much scrappy repartee ensues in the manner of a '40s-style romantic comedy ... The filmmakers have been inspired by the relationship between Tracy and Hepburn, but the pairing instead calls up visions of David Brinkley nibbling Tabitha Soren's little pink ear. Nolte looks as if he's making out with his niece."

Meanwhile, everything seemed great between Julia and Lyle. According to him at the time, "We have been discussing having a child after Julia finishes [filming] *Mary Reilly*."

However, it was only one month after the

release of *I Love Trouble* that things would change forever.

During the filming of *Mary Reilly* in London, Julia struck up a friendship with one of her co-stars, 25-year-old Michael Sheen, who played the role of Bradshaw in the film. When she flew him to New York City with her for a brief vacation, the press had a field day.

Lyle philosophically claimed, "Life is a lot more normal than what people might think from keeping up with the tabloid media. I'm just really happy to be in a great relationship."

However, the couple's relationship was doomed, on hindsight, from the very beginning. Although Julia had claimed that she wanted to start a family with Lyle, in reality they were rarely together. She was perpetually on movie sets and he was busy touring the countryside with his band. Furthermore, Lyle had at least one extramarital affair.

Suddenly, Julia Roberts and Lyle Lovett announced that they were getting a divorce. They had been married in June 1993 and they officially called it quits in July 1994.

Julia admitted to *People* magazine, "We were pretending to be a normal couple." Yet, she had to reluctantly concede: "Things don't always come out as you intended."

The divorce wasn't to become legally final until March 28, 1995, but they were off in separate directions by the second half of 1994.

That fall, while still legally married to Julia, Lyle was seen in a hotel with 25-year-old country singer Kelly Willis in October 1994. According to reports, they spent 12 hours together in Lyle's Austin, Texas, hotel room.

Although her marriage to Lyle was over, the couple miraculously remained very close friends. According to her, "Nobody could ask for a split up and be happier with one another. It's actually ridiculously amicable. It's sort of stupid. You'd think people who could be that nice to each other could probably be a couple. But it just sort of wasn't the way it was intended to be. We found our niche and then overstepped it."

Explaining the divorce, she said, "It's really our situation, and why it was, and why it wasn't is unique to us. They are situations that can be summed up in a sound bite. But I will say that with Lyle and myself, we opted for a real power move, which was the decision to split up. It was the strong choice as opposed to the weak choice. When people look at relationships, they think that to stay in a relationship, to work on it, is to be strong and to give up on it is really weak ... I know that I am a strong person. I know that I'm not a person who can do something and not do it fully. I know that I am a person of great convictions. And I have a very close relationship with Lyle Lovett. It's not going to just go away."

The press started to talk about Julia's relationship roulette as "the Velcro Syndrome." In other words, she was easily tightly attached to her beaus and just as instantly able to unattach herself.

She was a bit defensive about her whole experience with Lyle. "I think I'm better for having gone through everything that I went through. I fully believe in love and I fully believe in the interaction of people and the tangled mess that we can all get ourselves into. It serves a great purpose, whether it ends up positively or not. I mean, I believe in the experience."

Magazines and newspapers had a field day with the breakup, reporting trouble in paradise weeks before it was publicly official. Was she bothered by this? "I never gave it any thought," she said. "People say a lot of things. Once in a while, they're bound to be right, because usually what they're saying is negative and as life takes its course, some negative events will occur in your life."

Her brief marriage to Lyle wasn't a sore point for her. She looked at it as more than an adventure. "[It] served a lovely and important purpose for me," Julia explained. "The intricacies of it? The ins and outs of it? They really aren't anybody's business. I say as much as I can, because I try to be—for whatever stupid reason—a person who answers the questions asked. I do try to be accommodating. But it's hard, because there comes a point where I realize that it's OK for me to draw the line. We got along really well. We were married for a time. We're not married now. And, we're friends." Could it be any easier than that? She seemed as cool as a cucumber.

One day, not long after the divorce, Julia was in a store with her sister Lisa and all of a sudden Lyle's music and voice began playing in the shop. She recalls, "We both just sort of looked at each other—and went on buying lip balm or whatever the hell we were doing. And then I walked out of the store and I was like, 'Jesus! That on top of the rest of my day.' "

Her marriage to Lyle made her take a good long look at herself and her personal life. "Well, there is, oh, a sacredness to the personal relationship I have with Lyle, the details of which belong to us. But I will say that a real turning point for me as a person on this planet was when Lyle and I split up. It was recognizing the strength in the decision, owning the decision and not feeling bad or embarrassed or ashamed because the marriage didn't work out. We get along like a house on fire and he has taught me so many things. The relationship, more than anything, taught me to take responsibility for who I am. I mean, who am I to think I'm so special that I'm not allowed to make mistakes? When did I come up with that? So I am full and totally culpable for all of my errors, but that also forces me to find confidence enough to say that I am also fully responsible for all the wonderful success of my life, personal and professional. And that's a huge thing. Even right now, talking about this, my face is so hot, because it's hard to say."

She also found that she was getting more used to having her deepest, darkest, most personal relationship details publicly discussed. "Before, if somebody would bring up Kiefer, I'd be so embarrassed and you don't know what to say other than just, 'Well, you know ...' And you sort of try to make excuses for yourself and for the other person. And you know what? I don't do that anymore. It was what it was and it served a great purpose. I was able to extract the good out of the bad."

Julia was also happy about the way her career was going. "I like the jobs I get. I like the people I've had the chance to work with. I think I'm probably at my best. Just at my most collected. Happy for no major reason. I'm not happy because, I'm just happy," she said.

She was also feeling less and less competitive with the Sandra Bullocks and the Nicole Kidmans. Julia explains, "I'm not a competitive person. I believe that there's enough work to go around. When I first started off, and I wouldn't get a part—which happened frequently—when I would hear who got it, I'd be the first to go, 'Well, of course! She's much more suited for that than I am! It wasn't like, 'Oh that bitch!'"

We are all human, however, and although Julia had a reputation for always being sparkling on the set, she is the first to admit that she isn't always Mary Sunshine. "We all have our bad days. I've had crew guys that were friends of mine say, 'Whoooo! What was going on? You came barreling in there so pissed off!' Well, I was mad and I was cold and I was having a hard time. It's never directed toward anybody. I think I've twice, in eight years, given someone a complete

lashing. But I will also say this: I was upset
and I'm a person who has to express myself
or else I become paralyzed in a working
situation. When you feel utterly disappointed by someone that you have to see every
day, you have to tell them."

Wanting to let off some steam after the
pressures of her very public crumbling marriage to Lyle, she went out on the town with
actor Ethan Hawke. The star of such movies
as *Dead Poet's Society* and *Reality Bites*, for a
while, he was the perfect tonic for her to get
over Lovett. According to one of Roberts'
friends, "Julia was feeling lonely and
depressed at the time and Ethan was like taking a happy pill. He was somebody who
cheered her up." Julia claimed that her relationship with Ethan was nothing more than a
friendship. "I danced, was that a felony?" she
defensively stated at the time after being
spotted painting the town in Manhattan with
Hawk. "The facts are simple. I, actually for
the first time in a long time, went out to dinner. Just me with some people I've worked
with. Talked about some writers, everything
is going gangbusters. The band strikes up:
'Hey, you want to dance?' We all had a good
time. So, since when is that bad? I love to

dance. And I will continue to dance. In fact, I will just say right here and now that up until the time I go to work—and maybe after I'm already at work—I plan doing as much dancing with as many people as possible. I will dance until I drop. How about that?"

Whatever the nature of their relationship, it didn't last long. Julia herself was able to look back on her fling with Hawke and comment, "Ethan has come along at the worst possible time. It's sad because he wants something much more serious than I do." It wasn't long before the affair came to a sudden end.

Getting back to work, Roberts chose for her next role a comedy/drama called *Something to Talk About*. Originally, it was going to be entitled *Grace Under Pressure* and it seemed like the perfect choice for her. The executive producer on this film was Goldie Hawn. At the helm was Lasse Halström, who directed *What's Eating Gilbert Grape*, and it was written by the Oscar-winning screenplay writer of *Thelma & Louise*, Callie Khouri.

It is the story of Grace (Julia Roberts), a modern Southern woman who—on the surface—has it all. She has a cute and sharp daughter (Haley Aull)—whom she refers to as "Doodlebug," a handsome husband named Eddie (Dennis Quaid) and a pair of loving parents—Georgia and Wyly (Gena Rolands and Robert Duvall). She also has a great job raising prize racehorses. However, it all changes when she finds that Eddie is having an affair with a certain blonde in town. In fact, Grace spots him in public, kissing the other woman. Not one to hold her feelings inside, she confronts him in the middle of a local restaurant.

Instead of turning the other cheek, she has a sense of wounded pride—and according to her—that's the end of her marriage.

She becomes even more scalding when, at a meeting of the local women, she is informed that one of the members also slept with Eddie. When the moderator at the meeting asks for any new business, Grace stands up and asks, "I was just wondering if anyone else here has f***ed my husband?"

Something to Talk About is a cute film with strong character performances to keep the action going. However, it failed to have that special something that would have taken it over the top.

When *Something to Talk About* debuted in theaters in August 1995, it received generally good reviews. In *The Los Angeles Times*,

Kenneth Turan claimed, "*Something to Talk About* is like a slow-simmering stew, the kind that flavors familiar ingredients with special herbs and spices. Those spices surely accomplish wonders, but underneath it all you are left with the usual culinary suspects ... a fine cast, starting with star Julia Roberts ... *Something to Talk About* is at its best when Khouri's juicy script is adroitly mixing comedy and pathos ... when is Julia Roberts going to allow herself to smile more than briefly in a major motion picture? Although it is heartening to see her involved with this kind of quality material, her long-ago sunniness remains a distant memory."

According to Mick LaSalle of *The San Francisco Chronicle*, "In *Something to Talk About* we see a new Julia Roberts. For one thing, she doesn't do the smile except once, in the movie's last second ... *Something to Talk About* is European in its sprawl. Several side stories are simultaneously pursued and time is taken to get to know these people. The results are some powerful scenes. When Roberts and Dennis Quaid, as the estranged couple, meet over dinner and talk about their lives and their disappointments in marriage, there's almost a sense of eavesdropping. ... *Something to Talk About* never goes bad, though it does get corny in places."

With *Something to Talk About*, Julia Roberts at least pleased her fans with an engaging comedy. Now she was ready for new adventures and new challenges.

While in Europe in the fall of 1995 to film an upcoming Woody Allen comedy, Julia embarked on a series of adventures—of the romantic kind. First, she had a flirtation with Mario Fontanella, a 28-year-old gondola driver in Venice, Italy. She reportedly was seen dining with him and taking candlelit nighttime cruises through the canals.

She met Fontanella when he drove her via motorboat from her hotel, The Gritti Palace, to the film set. His other job was as a gondolier on the romantic canals of Venice. On Sept. 13, 1995, it was Fontanella who delivered Julia to her hotel. The following morning, Roberts protested when a different boat driver showed up to ferry her about. According to one report, "We had to go to Mario's apartment to get him out of bed to go fetch Julia. He really loved the attention."

Her bodyguard in Venice was a handsome hunk by the name of Lorenzo Slavan. Julia was also reportedly seen dining with Slavan at a restaurant in his hometown of Mestre on four consecutive nights. When she arrived in Paris for further filming, she was, again, in the company of Slavan. She also took him on a skiing excursion in the Italian Alps. According to all of these reports, she certainly wasn't lamenting the recent demise of her marriage. Soon enough, her European excursion was over and it was time to go back to Los Angeles where she was just about to start her next high-profile love affair.

CHAPTER SEVEN

Friends, Lovers & Dark Characters

I t was in November 1995 that Julia Roberts first became friends with one of the stars of the top-rated TV show, *Friends*. Reportedly, she had developed something of a crush on one of the show's stars, Matthew Perry. According to one report, "She had her agent pull some strings and get hold of Matt through his agent. Matt and Julia talked on the phone—and began a fax relationship.

She faxed him in Los Angeles, from her home in New Mexico and her apartment in New York, sending him flirty come-ons."

The two of them began faxing love notes back and forth to each other. "I love a man who can fax me five times in one day," was one of Julia's facsimile messages to Perry. It was Matthew's idea for her to be a guest star on the show. The producers of *Friends* loved the idea and soon an all-star special edition of the show was born.

On Dec. 19, 1995, Julia showed up at the *Friends* set unexpectedly. It was the last day before the show's Christmas break. She wasn't expected to come to the set until early January to tape her episode, but wanted to surprise Matthew.

She came to the Warner Brothers' lot dressed in sweatpants, her hair pulled back into a ponytail and she wore no makeup. She went directly over to Matthew Perry. According to a source on the set, "Matt's family was in town for Christmas and went to the set a lot. Julia went straight up to them and started chatting and laughing. It seemed like they'd met before. His mother really likes Julia, which is important to Matt because he is very close to him family. Matt and Julia were larking around like teenagers. There was a lot of pushing and playful shoving. But they were also very shy and coy toward each other and it appeared their relationship was very new."

Claimed the same source, "Matt couldn't believe that Julia was interested in him. When the faxes started coming through, he thought it was just a big joke, a hoax. When he discovered that it was really her, he flipped. They started having three-hour-long phone calls and got into a lot of romantic stuff you wouldn't normally see until a couple got together. They would talk about long walks in the rain and gushy stuff like that. Matt said she was incredibly funny. That impressed him a lot. It was her sense of humor that really won him over."

On Sunday, Jan. 28, 1996, Julia's episode of *Friends* aired. The special was an hour-long broadcast right after the Super Bowl. The episode also guest starred Brooke Shields, Chris Isaak and Jean-Claude Van Damme. It was such a highly promoted episode that the usual 30-second advertising rate was raised from $400,000 to $600,000.

In the first half of the show, Joey (Matt LeBlanc) discovers that he has his very own stalker (Brooke Shields). She finds it

From little girl to Pretty Woman: Julia Roberts at 9, 16 and 17, just before she realized her dream of becoming an actress.

Family Feud: Despite Eric Roberts helping his sister to land her first movie role, the two siblings fought bitterly.

> *"I'm too tall to be a girl,
> I never had enough dresses
> to be a lady, I wouldn't call
> myself a woman. I'd say
> I'm somewhere between a
> chick and a broad."*

**Mystic Pizza, a coming-of-age story based in a seaside
community in Connecticut, launched the careers of
Annabeth Gish, Lili Taylor and Julia Roberts.**

Mother and daughter – Betty Motes appears with Julia at a Young Actors' Gang fund-raiser.

The actress played Shelby in Steel Magnolias.

After co-starring with Dylan McDermott in Steel Magnolias and getting engaged, Julia suddenly called the marriage off.

Box-office magic: Richard Gere and Julia Roberts combined talents in Pretty Woman to rake in nearly $200 million worldwide.

Julia comforts her co-star Kiefer Sutherland in Flatliners. In real life, she would drop him just days before their scheduled wedding.

In Sleeping With the Enemy, the actress starred with Patrick Bergin to explore the dark side of abusive relationships.

The rising star brought a breath of fresh air to the dark subject matter of Dying Young (above) and laughs it up with Steven Spielberg on the set of Hook (below) in which she played Tinkerbell.

"*My real hair color is kind of dark blonde. Now I just have mood hair.*"

With blond hair and a million-dollar smile, Julia appeared on the arm of Kiefer Sutherland at the 63rd annual Academy Awards in L.A.

*As Kiefer Sutherland moved out of her house,
the actress was seen with Jason Patric.*

"This is completely right," said Julia of her marriage to country singer Lyle Lovett. Despite this appearance on stage with her new husband on their wedding night, the couple would divorce before celebrating a second anniversary.

Following her divorce from Lyle Lovett, Julia briefly romanced Ethan Hawke. "He wants something much more serious than I do," she announced after moving on.

> "I enjoy hats. And when one has filthy hair, that's a good accessory."

The actress uses her star power in a 6-day visit to Haiti as a goodwill ambassador for UNICEF.

After exchanging "love faxes" for weeks, Friends star Matthew Perry and Julia became an item.

Making working out fun, Julia dated her personal trainer Pat Manocchia for close to a year.

"I was thrilled to pieces to get to do something where no one was at any point going to say, 'Could you just give us a smile?'" Julia said about her role in Mary Reilly, with co-star John Malkovich.

Julia sang the ballad "All of My Life" in the Woody Allen musical comedy, Everyone Says I Love You.

Wild child Julia removes her bra to add to the celebrity collection at the bar Hogs & Heifers (above) and mixes it up with the locals (right).

*Drinking and romance mixed with Ross Partridge,
the bartender Julia dated in 1997.*

Mel Gibson and Julia joined forces in the thriller Conspiracy Theory.

"I've sort of grown into my cuteness."

"You'd think it was like chinchilla I had under there the way the world responded!" said Julia, after posing at the Academy Awards with her unshaved armpits.

Shades of Truth: Julia played an actress overwhelmed with her celebrity status and trying to find true love with Hugh Grant in Notting Hill.

On the red carpet – Julia meets her fans for a premiere.

Like the character she played in Runaway Bride,
Julia has left behind her own trail of broken hearts.

"When you live your life at that level of fame, it gets beyond your control," said Benjamin Bratt of Julia's suffocating stardom and his decision to end their relationship.

Brad Pitt and Julia teamed up South of the Border in The Mexican.

Julia takes a break from the cameras to spend time with her niece, Emma.

John Cusack and Catherine Zeta-Jones look to Julia Roberts to save the day in America's Sweetheart.

George Clooney and the actress caused the Hollywood rumor mill to churn by spending plenty of time away from the set during filming of Ocean's Eleven.

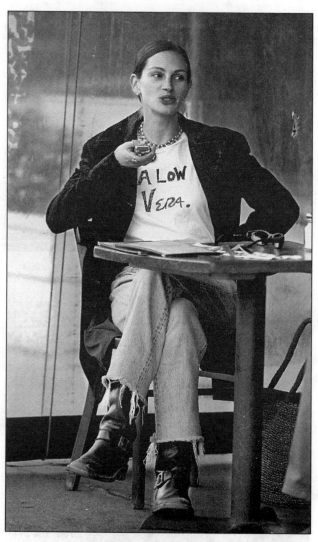

The movie star wears a T-shirt intended as a
potshot at Danny Moder's wife for delaying
signing the divorce agreement.

After meeting Danny Moder while filming The Mexican, Julia and the cameraman (left) married in a small ceremony at her New Mexico ranch July 4, 2002.

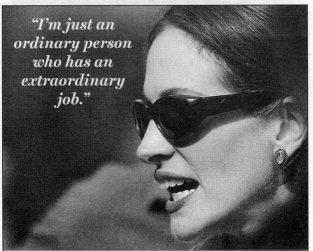

"I'm just an ordinary person who has an extraordinary job."

Julia attempts to settle into the routine of married life with Danny Moder in 2003.

absolutely impossible to differentiate the real-life Joey from his character of the doctor he plays on his TV soap opera. Meanwhile, off-key troubadour Phoebe (Lisa Kudrow) has her own fan. He (Chris Isaak) works at the New York Public Library on Fifth Avenue and he just happens to be looking for a singer to entertain children who are visiting the library. She flirts with him and gladly accepts the gig. However, her songs are totally inappropriate for children.

Meanwhile, Ross (David Schwimmer) visits the San Diego Zoo, only to find that his former pet, Marcel the monkey, was sold to movie producers and is now the star of the popular TV commercials for Monkey Shine Beer. He also finds out that Marcel is in New York City, acting in his first feature film, *Outbreak II: The Virus Takes Manhattan.*

When the *Friends* gang visits the movie set, Rachel (Jennifer Aniston) and Monica (Courteney Cox Arquette) fight over a date with Jean-Claude Van Damme. Chandler (Matthew Perry) runs into a makeup artist Susie Moss (Julia Roberts) with whom he attended the fourth grade. It seems that Susie remembers Chandler very well—as the boy who pulled her skirt up during the school play, exposing her panties to the entire audience. She has been harboring a grudge ever since. When he asks her out on a date, she says to him, "Maybe this time I'll get to see your underwear."

On their date, she provokes Chandler into wearing a pair of her girlish panties under his own pants while they go to a restaurant. Under the guise of having sex with him, she lures him to the restaurant bathroom and in a stall she instructs him to strip down to the panties. As he does so, she escapes with his clothes, leaving him to experience what it is like to be publicly humiliated. As she turns to exit the bathroom, she victoriously announces, "This is for the fourth grade!"

Later that year, however, the relationship started to show some strain. According to a colleague of Perry's, "Matt is worried she will dump him when it suits her. He knows how straining a Hollywood romance can be. I've heard him say how tough it is. He wonders how they can ever get their schedules together long enough to make it work."

Meanwhile, Julia had been signed to film *My Best Friend's Wedding*. As the leading man had yet to be chosen, Julia tried to persuade the producers into letting Matthew star in the film with her. They told her that he had no big-screen drawing power and turned down the idea flatly. This did nothing to help their budding relationship.

Also, the couple apparently got into some horrendous fights. Matthew was reportedly paranoid and jealous of Julia's relationship with Lyle Lovett. She would speak to Lyle on the phone while she was at Perry's house, setting off heated arguments.

Perry and Roberts seemed to have been genuinely happy with each other for a while, but just a quickly as it began, within months, it was all over. Julia Roberts was single again by the summer of 1996.

This was a period of exploration for Julia— she was ready to do something different. Tired of always having to be bubbly and smiling on screen, she chose to do one of her most serious and drab film portrayals, *Mary Reilly*. According to her at the time, "You don't want to do the same ol' thing. You want to try and mix it up a little bit."

To explain it further, she said: "I don't think I could play the character in *Pretty Woman* now. I'm a different person. I don't know if I could be that free or that whimsical, or that in-the-moment. But each thing I've done has come at a time when it represented a great challenge. *Mary Reilly* was certainly one of them."

Julia wanted a change of pace—and she got one with *Mary Reilly*. "This role does not call for any ounce of glamour I could ever possess," she said. "I was thrilled to pieces to get to do something where no one was at any point going to say, 'Could you just give us a smile?' "

To become the mousy and stoic maid to John Malkovich's twisted version of *Dr. Jekyll and Mr. Hyde*, Julia had to undergo a different kind of transformation. "I would go walking into the makeup room on *Mary Reilly* in a pair of overalls," she recalls, "and then I'd sit down and the next thing you know there's this whole different person."

A whole different person was what Julia was looking to become. It was to be her most extreme performance yet. Speaking about the fact that she was forever welded in the public mind to her *Pretty Woman* role, she claimed, "They've certainly embraced a particular persona of me—the whole *Pretty Woman* thing. But do I think that people want me to be the same all the time? No. They would get as bored of it as I would."

After many delays, *Mary Reilly* began production June 2, 1994. Principal photography was finished by September of that year. However, the director was not happy with the way the film ended, so in February 1995, both Julia Roberts and John Malkovich returned to Pinewood Studios in England and two more endings to the film were shot. In one version, Mary stays with Dr. Jekyll. In the second ending, Mary remains with Mr. Hyde. And in the third ending, Mary leaves them both.

Mary Reilly—and the book *Reilly*—is a retelling of Robert Louis Stevenson's terror classic, *Dr. Jekyll & Mr. Hyde*, reinterpreted to be seen from the perspective of the doctor's live-in chambermaid. Explaining the psyche of Mary Reilly's employer, Julia explains, "As two separate people, Dr. Jekyll and Mr. Hyde, they represent two very appealing facets of a relationship to Mary."

Of the character she portrays, Julia says, "She works for him from dawn 'til dusk and yet she's so happy to have this job, you know, and she is absolutely devoted to her employer, Dr. Jekyll. In her mind, Dr. Jekyll is this very intelligent, mysterious, almost magic figure."

As the plot develops, Mary becomes more entwined in her master's life and his experiments. "She is very curious as to what he does, what he is always doing. As her interaction with Dr. Jekyll increases, you see her feelings for him start to blossom."

With regard to what Dr. Jekyll has done in his transformation to Mr. Hyde, Julia explains, "What he has basically done is created a person who is without morals, who is without a conscience. This is beyond her realm of understanding. I mean, this poor girl has never been kissed. Dr. Jekyll is dealing with trying to possess a power and a knowledge which is unholy."

A repressed and confused girl, Mary Reilly is perplexed by the sexual advances on her by Hyde. She has no clue how to react to them, thanks to having been molested by her own father while she was just a child. In the end of the film, Hyde ends up killing Jekyll, as they vie for free rein in the same body. However, like the character of Mary Reilly herself, this film is oddly repressed and ultimately unsatisfying.

When *Mary Reilly* was released, the reviewing press universally disliked it. According to Liz Braun in *The Toronto Sun*, "Julia Roberts can't act (oh, get over it — she has) and John Malkovich never stops acting and as these two are the stars of *Mary Reilly* ... Glenn Close, apparently still in high *Sunset Boulevard* mode, shows up briefly to overact ... There's nothing wrong with the performances in this dark tale of a maid in the Dr. Jekyll/Mr. Hyde household. The movie doesn't work for entirely different reasons ... As a study of repression, *Mary Reilly* has some great moments, but it seems director Stephen Frears was aiming for intense and brooding, and boring is what he got."

Christine James of *Boxoffice Online Reviews* asked, "Is it a gothic horror? Is it a psychological thriller? Is it a love story? Ultimately, it seems the filmmakers don't even know the answer and as a result *Mary Reilly* doesn't succeed in any genre ... That a hairstyle keeps Mary from linking Hyde with Jekyll is as believable as Lois Lane not recognizing Superman because he's wearing glasses."

In the *Tucson Weekly*, Stacey Richter claimed, "The film is essentially a character study of Reilly, and the question is 'Why?' ... The story of *Mary Reilly* ... is slow, predictable and empty. Half of the movie is taken up by shots of Julia Roberts walking around in the fog ... what's the point?"

The best review that the film received came from Jim Ferguson of TV's *The Prevue Channel*. He called it "an old-fashioned, romantic, horror story with a terrific cast. It is Julia Roberts' most powerful performance in a love story with an unusual twist."

While critics and movie fans saw a brooding Julia Roberts on the screen in *Mary Reilly*, the real-life Roberts was busy kicking up her heels in public. Since her early 1996 affair with Matthew Perry wasn't working out, she was enjoying the company of her personal trainer, Pat Manocchia. In September 1996, she and Pat were seen partying in the Manhattan biker bar, Hogs & Heifers. A rowdy drinking establishment, Hogs & Heifers is known for its collection of brassieres from some of the most famous wild women in show business.

According to one eyewitness to Pat and Julia's late-night fun at the biker bar, "After they had a few beers, Julia slipped her bra out through one arm in her blouse and began to dance on the bar. At one point she even clenched her bra between her teeth as the crowd howled. She was having a great time, laughing and vamping with a barmaid. When she finished, Julia donated her bra to the bar, which has a sizable collection from other celebs including Drew Barrymore, Ashley Judd and Daryl Hannah." The source claimed that Julia and Pat partied until 4 in the morning. Hogs & Heifers' owner Allan Dell even posed for photographs with Julia's 34B-size bra. Apparently, everyone's favorite *Pretty Woman* could also be a wild woman when inspired.

There was nothing wild, however, about Julia's choice for her next film project. Like the dark and brooding *Mary Reilly*, the historical drama *Michael Collins* was equally dark, as well as moody.

On paper, *Michael Collins* must have seemed like a chance for Julia Roberts to co-star in a prestigious historical film with a sweeping and important message attached to it. However, the resulting film is dark, loses momentum somewhere in the middle and is—worst of all—completely uninspiring and ultimately confusing.

A film by Neil Jordan (*The Crying Game* and *Interview With a Vampire*), *Michael Collins* tackles a controversial story. It is the tale of a revolutionary by the name of Michael Collins (Liam Neeson), who begins the film as a clear-cut hero for the cause of an independent Ireland. However, in the middle of the film, when he is sent to London to negotiate a peace treaty, he comes back with a political compromise that has his own countrymen calling him a failure who sold-out his ideals.

A bleak and moody film, *Michael Collins*

doesn't properly explain why this cause of independence is significant or worthy of rooting for in one way or another. We see huge elaborate urban battles between the Irish revolutionaries and members of the British government, but the viewer is left not knowing what side to cheer for and for whom to jeer. We see one act of violence after another, but we couldn't care less who lives or who dies.

Furthermore, Julia's character of Kitty Kiernan is a dour and unhappy lass, with nothing much to do but be the occasional window dressing and sometime love interest of Michael Collins. Because the plot is so confusing, at several points in the film, words appear on the screen to explain what is going on historically. This is as good as sending up a white flag of defeat from the filmmakers. In the production notes, it is admitted that no one knows for sure who killed the real-life Michael Collins. Since the ending is unknown, the filmmakers simply made one up and then announce that this was the assumed conclusion of *Michael Collins*.

When *Michael Collins* was released in October 1996, the critics weren't kind. In *The San Francisco Examiner*, Barbara Shulgasser pondered, "The question is how do the Irish view Collins: As the fellow who bombed the British out of Ireland or as the one who insisted that the bombing he started must stop? Some Irish view both Collins and De Valera as sellouts." She also complained, "Jordan throws in a decorative Julia Roberts as a more or less unnecessary romantic involvement ... Jordan says he means to celebrate Collins 'the statesman and, ultimately, man of peace.' I'm not sure he succeeds ... Let's just say that *Michael Collins* is no *Lawrence of Arabia*."

Joseph McBride writing for *Box Office Magazine* succinctly pointed out, "Most viewers will have a hard time following Jordan's overly hasty and oblique narrative of the tortuous events of the Civil War and the Machiavellian intrigues of Collins' rival, Eamon de Valera." He also favored "less emphasis on the tepidly obligatory romantic subplot involving Julia Roberts as Collins' inamorata Kitty Kiernan."

Stacey Richter in *The Tucson Weekly* found that "the violence is graphic and it's hard at times to sympathize with our hero, Michael Collins, appealingly played as he is by Liam Neeson, because his special gift in life seems to be terrorism ... There's a silly love story with Julia Roberts thrown in for good measure and lots of explosions, if you get bored of the male bonding."

As much as the press jumped on her for doing *Mary Reilly* and *Michael Collins*, Julia Roberts continued to defend her career decisions. "I try to do different things. As much as a movie like *Mary Reilly* didn't do well, I loved being someone so totally different. People trashed it. They said, 'Well, she never smiled in the whole movie.' But isn't it OK to do something when there's not a lot to be happy about? Should I smile just because people want to see me smile? But on the other hand, if I kept on doing romantic comedies after *Pretty Woman*, kept on smiling and having fun, people would be like, 'Gag! Enough! Do Something! Tell a story!' It's an interesting 'Catch-22.'"

Garry Marshall defended her career choices as well by stating, "She wants to be risky, be brave, not just make franchise movies. She's very serious about acting. The critic who didn't like *Mary Reilly* will be long gone and Julia Roberts will still be working."

Shedding a little more light on the subject Julia claimed, "I had some hard times when I started making movies with people taking advantage of their authority and I didn't defend myself—which anyone who knows me now would think, 'Yeah, right.' But I didn't have the skills to confront people. It's got something to do with wanting to be a Southern girl, wanting to keep things nice and placid."

Who would have guessed that her next film was going to be something completely out of left field for her—a musical!

CHAPTER EIGHT

Everyone Says I Love Julia

As she was preparing to do her next film, *Everyone Says I Love You*, Julia was asked to explain the plot of it. According to her, "It's a Woody Allen movie. Quite frankly, all I feel that needs to be said is that it's a Woody Allen movie."

Everyone Says I Love You was mainly marketed as an art film and it received great reviews as one of the most ambitious of

Woody's films. It was his first attempt at making an out-and-out musical comedy. Like so many of the great comedies from the 1930s, the central characters in this film are all wealthy, living together in a Park Avenue apartment.

The patriarch of the film is Bob Dandridge (Alan Alda), who is a successful businessman. His wife, Steffi (Goldie Hawn) is a society woman who immerses herself in various charity projects. Since Bob is Steffi's second husband, some of the children in the household are from her first marriage to Joe Berlin (Woody Allen). The Dandridge offspring include optimistic Schuyler (Drew Barrymore), competitive sisters Lane (Gaby Hoffman) and Laura (Natalie Portman), overly serious son Scott (Lukas Haas) and wise-cracking D.J. (Natasha Lyonne).

Joe Berlin is the typical neurotic New Yorker that Woody usually plays in his films. He now lives in Paris, but shows up in Manhattan long enough to kvetch about his doomed interpersonal relationships.

Amid all of this, everyone is singing and dancing up a storm in several choreographed musical numbers. A huge admirer of the films of the Marx Brothers and Fred Astaire and Ginger Rogers, Woody Allen has taken many a cue here from their classic 1930s movies. Fortunately, the plot and the film's tone are so light, that it does not seem at all disrupting when a cast member suddenly bursts into song and dance. Along the way there are some great musical numbers, including one in Harry Winston's jewelry boutique, with Edward Norton warbling his way through *My Baby Just Cares for Me*.

This is a cast populated with actors who are not necessarily known for their singing. Julia Roberts however, tackled her first singing role head-on. With the ballad *All My Life*, her voice is a bit thin and plaintive, but she pulled it off quite successfully. Surprisingly, it is Alan Alda and Goldie Hawn who have the best voices.

When *Everyone Says I Love You* opened in January 1997, the critics loved it. It became a small cult film, but not a huge blockbuster. It remains a little-known gem and the first and only Julia Roberts musical comedy.

Tom Lyons of *Eye Weekly* wrote, "The entire film, in fact, seems like an extension of the Marx Brothers routine glimpsed near the end of *Hannah and Her Sisters* ... but Allen saves the movie from being a tedious exercise in the obvious by drawing on a ludicrous cross-section of characters. The numerous love stories intertwine with each other in a dizzying fashion, but the effortless ensemble acting renders the confusion amusing rather than irritating."

Peter Travers of *Rolling Stone* was particularly charmed by the film, claiming, "For Woody Allen in *Everyone Says I Love You*, the heart is the key to reinvigorating the musical. Allen says he doesn't care whether the actors in his film can sing or dance: Feeling is what counts ... Joe's latest is Von (a lovely Julia Roberts) ... *Everyone Says I Love You* proves the musical can still cut it as sublime entertainment. Woody, may the Force be with you."

Roger Ebert in *The Chicago Sun-Times* wrote, "Sometimes, when I am very happy, I sing to myself. Sometimes, when they are very happy, so do the characters in *Everyone Says I Love You*, Woody Allen's magical new musical comedy. I can't sing. Neither can some of Allen's characters. Why should that stop them? Who wants to go through life not ever singing? Here is a movie that had me with a goofy grin plastered on my face for most of its length ... One of the movie's loveliest moments, Allen singing *I'm Through With Love* on a balcony overlooking the Grand Canal. Of course he is not;

soon after, he sees the enticing Von (Julia Roberts) in Venice and falls in love at first sight ... I thought that perhaps *Everyone Says I Love You* is the best film Woody Allen has ever made. Not the most profound or the most daring or the most successful in every one of its details—but simply the best."

Reviews weren't the only interesting thing in Julia Roberts' life hitting the press. One of the most interesting things being reported was the long-running feud between Julia Roberts and her older brother Eric. In the early 1990s, Eric had developed a drug and alcohol problem and it was believed that his substance abuse issues were the reason for the siblings being on odd footing with each other. Eric later became clean and sober. However, it came to light that this was not just a lifestyle disagreement but a full-fledged family feud.

The battle between Julia and her brother continued to be a sore point—and it had been going on for 10 years. According to Eric in 1997, "Julie is on my mom's side in every family squabble. My mother and I do not get along. So, Julie and I don't get along. But I love her. I'll always love Julie. I think insecurities that she's just now coming to terms with can be traced back to her tough childhood where none of us got enough love. I'd love for it to change. Maybe one day it will."

According to Julia, "The thing is, we all have issues in our life—baggage that we inherit from our families. And I've sort of gotten to a place where I'm dealing with them and resolving them. I've put a lot of effort into fixing it. But eventually you get to a place where you're at peace with the fact that you're not smart enough to fix something that you don't really understand."

Speaking or not, her brother Eric did note that she had grown immensely as a person lately. "The old Julie was always concerned about making impressions. I understand that she's really self-confident these days. Good for her. Must be the result of hard work on herself."

Meanwhile, Julia was preparing for the release of her next hit comedy film. Screenplay writer Ron Bass is the man responsible for the script of *My Best Friend's Wedding*. The inspiration came from the wedding of one of his friends, which he attended. "It was a gigantic affair, in a splendid city, with all these people united in celebrating the happiness of the couple," he recalls. "It was so perfect, I just fantasized about this Lucy Ricardo kind of character dropping into the middle of the joy, determined to gum up the works, absolutely convinced she's on the side of right as she lies, cheats, steals, does whatever she must do to stop the affair."

Julia loved the script, explaining, "It's really hard to find an interesting, good, original comedy, period. They're just sort of rather impossible to come across and I think that I was so overjoyed, because I like doing comedy and so this one was very appealing to me."

Principal photography commenced June 19, 1996, in Chicago. Several famous sites were used to give the film a lot of color and character. One scene took place at Cominskey Park at a White Sox baseball game. According to Dermot Mulroney the baseball spectators that day "were doing their level best to get Julia to raise her T-shirt. They were like: 'Hey, Juuuulia! This Bud's for you!' then they all raised their shirts and showed her their sunburned bellies." Julia thought it was positively hysterical. She yelled back at the fans, "StttairMaster!"

In *My Best Friend's Wedding*, Julia Roberts plays Julianne "Jules" Potter. It is three weeks before her 28th birthday and she is an influential Manhattan food critic.

When she was in college, her best friend was Michael O'Neal (Dermot Mulroney) and they made a pact with each other: If both of them were single when they reached the age of 28, they would marry each other. When Michael suddenly phones her, she assumes it is to propose marriage. She is, however, dumbfounded to find out that he has rung her up to invite her to his wedding—as he has met someone and fallen in love.

Like a bull with a red cape waved in front of it, Jules runs to Chicago on a mission: She has four days to steal the groom away from his new fiancée. The first problem is the fact that the bride-to-be is perfectly charming. Cameron Diaz plays the other woman, Kimmy, with a sense of doe-like innocence that is hard not to find charming. But a mission is a mission and Jules embarks on her own agenda of lying, deceit and comically backfiring underhanded deeds.

With *My Best Friend's Wedding*, Julia Roberts finally had another runaway blockbuster box-office hit on her hands. After a pair of films that everyone seemed to hate— *Michael Collins* and *Mary Reilly*—Julia was back on top!

Furthermore, the critics loved it. William

Thompson adored the film and wrote in his review in *The Anchorage Press*, "It's funny, it's emotional and it temporarily cures narcolepsy ... In addition to the flawless performances of all four principles, P.J. Hogan has directed well beyond the promise of *Muriel's Wedding* ... [*My Best Friend's*] *Wedding* has the most wit, spice, and impeccable narrative structuring."

Ruthe Stein in *The San Francisco Chronicle* glowed of Julia, "The actress is at her vibrant best—a pretty woman again instead of the pale imitation in recent films like *Mary Reilly* and *Michael Collins*. [P.J. Hogan] knows how to show his star off, putting her in almost every scene and keeping the camera on her ... There is an actor who is every bit a match for Roberts—Rupert Everett, playing Julianne's editor and confidant, George."

Roger Ebert in *The Chicago Sun-Times* found it fun to not be rooting for Julia's character to win: "Julianne gets the idea of forging an e-mail from Kimmy's rich dad to the editor of Michael's sports magazine. The e-mail is the movie's turning point ... That makes the third act surprisingly interesting: We don't have any idea what will happen ... Roberts, Diaz and

Mulroney are in good synch and Roberts does a skillful job of negotiating the plot's twists."

The Boston Globe loved her performance, raving, "In *My Best Friend's Wedding* she's a stitch as a witch. Julia Roberts is a little older, a little more aware of how to make an out-of-control quality work for her."

The film proceeded to take in a reported $21.5 million on the first weekend it opened in June 1997. By the time it was finished, the film grossed $120 million. Julia Roberts was back in the winner's circle. The following January, her portrayal of "Jules" in *My Best Friend's Wedding* was nominated for a Golden Globe Award in the category of Best Actress in a Comedy or Musical.

Julia was about to begin one of her longest relationships. It came about via a chance meeting. In fact, she was in a restaurant in October 1997 when she spotted Benjamin Bratt, one of the stars of the TV show *Law & Order*.

Benjamin remembers, "I walked into a restaurant one night and Julia was there with a group of friends celebrating her birthday. The maitre d' came over and said 'Julia Roberts wants to buy you a drink.' It's a restaurant I frequent and I thought one of my friends was playing a joke on me, so I walked out without saying a word to her."

The following day, he discovered that it actually had been the real Julia Roberts who offered him a drink. He quickly penned a note to her and patched up the mistake of the unintentional snub.

She accepted his apology and they began a very hot and heavy affair, which was to last for four years. One of the most interesting things that happened was that the paparazzi and the press seemed to give the couple more space and privacy than she had been used to in the past.

Julia jokingly theorized, "I think he's just a badass and everybody's scared. But as a team, I think we've done very well dealing with the attention and I also think that people, for whatever reason, are more respectful than they used to be."

Regarding the large role her ex-husband still played in her life, she explains, "I have what I call the Lyle barometer. If a guy cannot deal with the fact that Lyle and I are such good friends, then OK, we just don't go any further. And if you're secure in yourself and you really want happiness for this person that you love, then it's not a hard thing to do. I'm here to tell you, I have a pretty good example of that [with Benjamin]. Because if you really love someone you wouldn't say, 'I want you to be happy, but could you remove this person from your life?' Well, then, why not say, 'Get rid of your couch and, while you're at it, don't wear that top anymore.' It's that same crap which is their insecurity. So, no, no, no. No more time for that in my life. Those days are over."

While all of this went on, Julia was busy working on her next film. When they were working together on the film *Assassins*, Brian Helgeland was asked by producer Joel Silver if he had any new screenplay ideas. Helgeland informed him, "There's a paranoid guy who prints his own newsletter called Conspiracy Theory in which he exposes so-called conspiracies. What would happen if he accidentally got one right? He's The Boy Who Cried Wolf and when he accidentally gets one right, the wolves show up."

He also had another film idea. It was a love story where two people could never get the relationship off the ground in spite of their love for each other.

Explains Helgeland, "It dawned on me one day that I should combine the two stories. What works well in this film is that you have this big world of conspiracy theories and in the middle of that arena, you have this guy who's hopelessly in love with this woman. That is the heart of the whole movie." And so, *Conspiracy Theory* was born.

The producers of the film instantly interested Mel Gibson in playing the role of Jerry. "I found the subject matter intriguing," he claims. "As far as conspiracy theories go, I give some credence to them. I have no doubt that there's a covert force at work somewhere, keeping things undercover and admitting only certain things to the public."

It was Mel Gibson who came up with the idea of having Julia Roberts play the role of Alice in the film. "The material was easy to say 'yes' to," recalls Julia. "But I had just finished a movie and I didn't want to work. So, Joel, Dick and Mel trapped me in a hotel room and wouldn't let me leave until I said 'yes.'"

According to her, "As soon as I agreed, they had a brass band march out and play me a victory song I figured I had just made a decision that I knew wouldn't be boring, ever!"

Mel Gibson would later claim that he got along great with Julia Roberts. "She's generally friendly. When she comes on the set and asks, 'How are my men doing this morning?' all the grips and electricians just melt."

At face value, Mel Gibson as Jerry is a paranoid nut job. A babbling cab driver afraid of his own shadow who thinks that everything is a government conspiracy. He picks up riders in his cab and either frightens them or bores them with his non-stop monologues. He also publishes a regular Conspiracy Theory newsletter to a select mailing list. Of course, in the twists and turns of Hollywood, just because you're paranoid doesn't mean that someone isn't out to get you.

Jerry is also obsessively stalking Julia Roberts' character, Alice Sutton. Alice is a government agent in the Justice Department. When Jerry demandingly visits Alice's office, he informs her of his various theories—from presidential assassinations to surveillance helicopters flying overhead. As big a wacko as Jerry is, there is something somehow charming about him and Alice begins to see this through his manic daftness.

Naturally, one of Jerry's rambling theories is totally on target. When he is kidnapped, tortured and shot up with truth serum, the plot really kicks into full gear. As a smoothly intelligent criminal, Patrick Stewart is evil perfection.

When Jerry escapes, he runs to the one person who he trusts—Alice. What started out like a kooky caper film now races into full-fledged adventure flick mode as the plot just continues to thicken. *Conspiracy Theory* has some great chase scenes and the right amount of suspense to carry the unlikely plot twists and keep the audience guessing. Julia plays her role with a stylish coolness and is appealingly self-confident.

When *Conspiracy Theory* was released in August 1997, the American critics were decidedly mixed on the results. In *The Anchorage Press*, William Thompson called it "an intriguing, yet flat-footed rendition of the hysterical lust for confirmation of external forces controlling our lives. It's more likely 'lust' and not 'external forces' driving this conspiracy of conspiracy-based entertainment, when beautiful people like Mel Gibson and Julia Roberts are involved ... This film tries to balance true paranoia with comedy, thus failing in comparison to the masterpieces of the genre, including *Manchurian Candidate* ... Even with the inept synthesis of paranoia and comedy, *Conspiracy Theory* would have rated one moose higher if it had not put love into the melee." Still, he found "*Conspiracy Theory* is worth watching."

In *The San Francisco Examiner*, Barbara Shulgasser claimed that *Conspiracy Theory* was a "well-written thriller graced by good humor and fine acting ... As in all the good thrillers—*Charade, North by Northwest, To Catch a Thief*—nothing is what it seems ... Roberts has matured much in the past few years ... Roberts has learned that seriousness doesn't rule out humor, so she allows that wonderful spark of hers, that sharp skepticism and tendency to laugh first and ask questions later, to come through and abide comfortably beside her warmth and femininity. This is an extremely good performance from an actress who gets better every time out."

However, in *The San Francisco Chronicle*, Mick LaSalle complained, "If I were paranoid I might suspect a conspiracy at work in the promoting of this movie—to suck in audiences with a catchy hook ... Roberts has lost her two least appealing tendencies—to preen and to act all bothered and put-upon at the slightest provocation. She's more believable here, both as a lawyer and as a compassionate person willing to tolerate Fletcher ... But it's just a simple thriller whose goal is little more than to keep moving." Although he despised the plot, LaSalle pointed out, "When all else fails, there are still the stars to look at — Roberts, who actually manages to do some fine acting and Gibson, whose likability must be a sturdy thing indeed."

In addition to everything else that she was involved in, 1998 found Julia Roberts in the PBS-TV special *In the Wild: Orangutans with Julia Roberts*. It was part of the acclaimed PBS series, *Nature*. In it, the actress travels to exotic Borneo in search of the last surviving apes of the continent of Asia. In the special, Julia is seen as the hostess and narrator.

However, the TV taping was not just a docile visit to the zoo. According to Julia, at one point on camera she was being introduced to a 400-pound orangutan who was known as "Kusai," and he grabbed her around the neck. He was just trying to become friendly, but Julia was terrified. "I thought he would probably end my life," she was later to recount. "My head was spinning and my heart—my microphone was in my bra—you can hear my heart start going faster and faster. It was sort of sensory overload."

She was quick to explain, "I don't want

people to think I'm wimpy. When they 'cut' I appear completely free, but in actuality one of Kusai's feet is holding onto my wrist below the frame."

She couldn't believe how large Kusai was. "You can't imagine how big he is unless you're really in front of him. Next to him, I look like I belong on a keychain! And, there I was trying to reassure him!"

From the hills of Hollywood to the wilds of Borneo, Julia Roberts was truly solidifying her reputation as the hardest-working actress in show business!

CHAPTER NINE

Runaway Hits

Julia's next film was 1998's highly successful *Stepmom*. She and her friend Susan Sarandon had been searching for a film that they could star in together and finally they found this dramatic comedy. According to producer Wendy Finerman, "Susan and Julia had both read the script and they were excited about it. Both are family-oriented and they loved the story. It suited them perfectly."

In *Stepmom*, Julia plays successful commercial photographer Isabel Kelly. She has unwittingly become the stepmother to two preteen children. They are the offspring of her boyfriend, Luke Harrison (Ed Harris) and his former wife, Jackie (Sarandon). They have the kids half of the week and Jackie has them the other half.

At first, the children—Anna and Ben (Jenna Malone and Liam Aiken)—don't like Isabel and Jackie does nothing to dissuade her children's attitudes. Clearly the children are being used as pawns in a failed marriage.

Isabel tries in her own charming way to win over the children. She buys them a puppy. She takes them on a big photo shoot in Central Park. When the little boy wanders off unattended, battle lines are draw between the mother and the stepmother.

By the time Luke asks Isabel to marry him, it is clear that she is not just a passing fancy in his life. From the middle of the film forward, Jackie has been putting up a good front, but she has kept a dark secret. She has been diagnosed with cancer and is not responding to the treatment. Toward the end of the film she finally has to come terms with the fact that it is Isabel who is going to be there for her children.

When it opened on Christmas day 1998, *Stepmom* drew mixed reviews. According to

Entertainment Weekly magazine, "Director Chris Columbus, whose talent for creating decorative gingerbread-house domestic comedies benefited *Home Alone* and *Mrs. Doubtfire*, takes an awful lot of pleasure in the girl-girl competition, encouraging the worst in Sarandon and Roberts."

Brenda Sokolowski of *The Anchorage Press* loved it and wrote, "I knew exactly what to expect when I walked into this movie ... But I never expected to like it. Shoot me; I liked it ... To her credit, Julia Roberts actually makes lines like "I really do have their best interests at heart" sound emotionally fresh. Susan Sarandon conveys all the hurt and maturity of a put-upon ex-wife."

Tucson Weekly thought that the same material could be better put to use in a better way and claimed, "Joan Collins and Linda Evans taught us how to take care of deep hatred when they had knockdown brawls on *Dynasty*. Sadly, but a decade later, Julia Roberts and Susan Sarandon have forgotten this very satisfying solution to sisterhood gone awry ... I'd rather stay home and watch Heather Locklear kick everybody's ass on *Melrose Place*."

Although some critics didn't care for the

sentimentality of this film, theater audiences' opinions differed and turned *Stepmom* into a big hit for Julia Roberts and her buddy Susan Sarandon.

After a couple of guest-starring roles on *Sesame Street* and her boyfriend Benjamin Bratt's popular series *Law & Order*, it was time again for another big movie project—this one called *Notting Hill*.

Julia confesses that when she first read the script for *Notting Hill*, she was uncertain of her own judgment, so she consulted Benjamin. She explains, "So I called my boyfriend and said, 'I think it's really funny, but I can't tell.' And he could appreciate by the tone of my voice how frenetic I was. So I sent it to him Johnny-on-the-spot and he read it just as quickly. And he called me up and said, 'That is the no-brainer of all time.'" She accepted the role.

The script for *Notting Hill* was written by Richard Curtis, who penned the popular *Four Weddings and a Funeral*—the movie that made Hugh Grant into a huge movie star. According to Curtis, the central idea behind *Notting Hill* came from a fantasy he had. He imagined what it would be like to show up at a dinner party given by his friends, and his date was Madonna or Princess Diana. The result of imagining that one situation was the genesis for what became *Notting Hill*.

Notting Hill is an absolutely perfect Julia Roberts film. She is funny, refreshing, totally vulnerable and delightful to watch in it. Furthermore, her on screen chemistry with Hugh Grant is wonderful. She is fiery and unpredictable, he is cool and centered, and together they play off of each other wonderfully. William Thacker (Hugh Grant) owns a small London store called the Travel Book Shop and Anna Scott (Julia Roberts) is—like her own real life—one of the biggest movie stars in the world. This film is as much a comically fictional tale, as it is a spoof on Roberts' own existence as a star.

When Anna wanders into the Travel Book Shop by chance, she is impressed by William's charm. After making her purchase, she leaves the shop assuming that she will never see him again. However, when William runs out to buy two take-out glasses of orange juice, he runs into Anna—literally—and soaks her with the beverages. Embarrassed, he invites her to his nearby flat to clean up.

As she is leaving his flat and they are saying goodbye again, she kisses him. It becomes clear that their paths are due to cross again.

William has a goofy roommate named Spike (Rhys Ifans), who has an inability to take telephone messages properly. William is horrified to find that Anna has been trying to get in touch with him. However, they eventually talk on the phone and Anna invites him to meet her at her hotel.

As Anna, Julia acts shy and charming. And as William, Hugh has an innocent quality that is easy for her to find irresistible. He asks her to dinner and she accepts. The ensuing dinner party is enchanting fun, with all of the guests tripping over themselves in an attempt not to make fools of themselves.

Clearly, love is blossoming between Anna and William. However, things hit the rocks when her American boyfriend (Alec Baldwin) shows up unexpectedly. When William later complains to his friends that he had no idea she had a boyfriend, they all roll their eyes, all having read about it in the gossip columns. William deadpans, "I don't believe it, my whole life ruined because I don't read *Hello* magazine!"

When it was released in May 1999, critics absolutely loved *Notting Hill*. Cindy Fuchs in *The Philadelphia City Paper* glowed of Julia's performance, "There's no argument

that Roberts plays this character well. And
there's no argument that in making Anna a
wild, unreal creature in need of taming and
realness, she follows a road map established
by the best of previous romantic comedy
heroines like Katharine Hepburn, Carole
Lombard, Molly Ringwald, Meg Ryan and
Roberts herself. As the *Pretty Woman*, after
all, she was nothing if not independent,
vulnerable, knowing, naive, erratic and
beguiling, not to mention eager to give it all
up for the man of her dreams. Clearly,
Roberts can play the version of herself with
which you're familiar and happy."

In *The Chicago Sun-Times*, Roger Ebert
wrote, "The movie is bright, the dialogue has
wit and intelligence, and Roberts and Grant
are very easy to like. By the end, as much as
we're aware of the ancient story machinery
groaning away below deck, we're smiling."

Kenneth Turan in *The Los Angeles Times*
liked the film as well: "Taking advantage of
Anna's star-of-stars status, some of *Notting
Hill's* funniest situations deal with the movie
business. While Grant wins us over immediately, Roberts has a tougher time. This is partly
because, despite the actress's insistence that
a picture about heroic nuns ministering to

lepers in equatorial Africa couldn't be further
from her life than this one, *Notting Hill* does
seem within at least shouting distance of a
self-portrait ... the film's romantic core is
impervious to problems. Roberts and Grant
are the most glowing of stars here, the people
who keep us alive in the darkness and we
want so much for their characters to be
happy in their turn."

Between *Stepmom* and *Notting Hill*, 1999
was an excellent year for Julia Roberts. With
both a drama and a comedy hit in the theaters
in rapid succession, she was feeling very
much on top of the world. The following
January, Julia was again nominated for a
Golden Globe Award, in the category of Best
Actress in a Comedy or Musical.

In addition to her career going well, she
seemed very happy in her relationship with
Benjamin Bratt. They both had busy careers,
but they enjoyed each other's company.
However, there were no wedding announce-
ments.

When her schedule permitted, she also
enjoyed some time off to herself. What does
Julia Roberts do when she has time on her
hands? Well that isn't very often, but she
takes full advantage of it. She gets to hang

out with her eight dogs—who are—so she claims, "all mutts, all from the pound."

She also takes advantage of the fact that she can "wake up when I want. Watch TV if I want. Pee when I want. And, see my family as often as I want."

In 1999 Julia admitted, "I went through sort of an elongated confidence dilemma. Even now, in a kind of absurd way, I still have an element of that. As if tomorrow they could say, 'OK, time's up. Go back to Smyrna.' You know. You find yourself sort of living out your dream and at the same time, you wonder how did you get here? Do you deserve to be here? Then you add in all the interviews and people taking your picture on the street and all that kind of stuff scared the s**t out of me. And when you're 21 years old, you're still trying get your own legs as just this gawky girl in the world."

According to her friend Susan Sarandon, "I don't know many 21-year-olds who really know who they are. But she emerged from that very complicated gestation period with a clear voice and a sense of who she is. I like her because Julia's someone who says 'yes' to life. She's funny and smart and fearless, and she's come through everything with so much confidence and grace, which is really the higher road. You can just as easily end up in the Betty Ford Clinic. I've seen it happen."

Regarding her self-confidence level, Julia admitted, "The thing that I'm able to do now is put words to the feelings, as opposed to once upon a time when if someone approached me in a certain way, I might just look at them and inside I'm thinking, 'Please, go away. Please, stop looking at me. Please, please, please, I don't know how to deal with you. I don't know what to do ...' But it was a challenge that obviously I had to have in my life and I think I was able to draw a lot of things from it. And I regret not a moment of it. Not even at its worst moment of really being apoplectic with ignorance, because my life now is so—I just live my life now. And each little stepping stone leads to the next thing and it sounds kind of corny but to remove one element of it is collapse the whole house of cards."

However, amidst all the happiness in Julia's life, there was an increasing pressure to replicate the success that she had with her all-time career high point—*Pretty Woman*. She scoffed at the notion of doing a sequel. *"The Return of Pretty Woman!"* she laughed. *"Prettier Woman! Prettier But Slightly Older Woman!*

Slightly Older But Still OK! I just think it was what it was and to try to make it more than what it was is asking for it," she hypothesized.

Although there would be no *Pretty Woman 2*, Julia's next film project found her co-starring with a familiar face—Richard Gere. Ultimately, it was Gere who first read the script that became the film *Runaway Bride*. He loved it and felt that it was something that might be good for the two of them to do together.

One of the most appealing aspects of doing *Runaway Bride* with the same leading man and director Julia had in *Pretty Woman* was the fact that Garry Marshall also employed several of the same character actors to populate this lighthearted comedy. Larry Miller, who was the shopkeeper who collected an "obscene" amount of cash from Gere and Roberts in *Pretty Woman*, turns up as the bartender in a New York watering hole. Hector Elizondo, who played the hotel manager in *Pretty Woman*, is seen here as Gere's friend and editor. And the big-eyed night elevator operator from *Pretty Woman*, Patrick Richwood, is seen here as one of the TV hosts at the big wedding.

Gere plays Ike Graham, a columnist for *USA Today*, working on a story about a woman who leaves her fiancé at the altar. The woman's name is Maggie Carpenter (Julia Roberts) and she has gone through three husbands-to-be and is now working on Number Four.

His newspaper publishes the story, but Maggie fires back such a burning letter to the newspaper that *USA Today* dumps him from their staff. Thanks to his buddy Fisher (Hector Elizondo), Ike places a freelance piece with *GQ* and then goes to Maggie's hometown to do some research.

As Ike interviews everyone Maggie knows for his magazine article, she begins to see his allure. However, she has fiancé Number Four to deal with first. Just like clockwork, she dumps Coach Bob Kelly (Christopher Meloni) and the path is clear for Ike to win her heart.

There is also a fifth wedding in the film— intended to be the union of Maggie and Ike. In an amusing sight gag, all of Ike's New York friends are sitting on one side of the church, all dressed in black and wearing dark sunglasses. Although *Runaway Bride* doesn't have the same magic sparkle as *Pretty Woman*, it has a lot of fun with this wedding-gone-awry premise.

When *Runaway Bride* hit theaters in

September 1999, the critics were mixed. Donna Bowman in *The Nashville Scene* was skeptical about the results of *Runaway Bride*. According to her, "America fell in love with Roberts already, but the producers seem to think we can still fall in love with Gere. Fat chance. He may be boinkable, but he's just not lovable ... Marshall makes frantic attempts to recreate some of the spontaneous delight that audiences remember from *Pretty Woman*. But every moment is forced, packaged with huge bows of sentiment; the result annoys the viewer like a dog begging for treats under the table. *Runaway Bride* wants to be a second honeymoon, but this marriage can't be saved."

Roger Ebert in *The Chicago Sun-Times* didn't care for it at all and proclaimed, "Movies like this should have an explanatory note at the outset, to help us understand them. Something like: The following characters all look really great but don't know anything they haven't learned by watching sitcoms. After seeing Gere and Roberts play much smarter people (even in romantic comedies), it is painful to see them dumbed down here."

Kenneth Turan in *The Los Angeles Times* found *Runaway Bride* successful on the surface, but was unable to erase the image of what a superior film *Pretty Woman* was. "Roberts, as she was in the more successful *Notting Hill*, is in full movie-star mode, lithe, smiling and game for all kinds of physical humor, including pratfalls and the making of comically ridiculous faces. This is all great fun, but Maggie is such a terrific person it doesn't really fit with the film's need to paint her, at least in part, as someone who has thoughtlessly ruined any number of lives ... In a movie filled with improbable sequences, this at least is one we're happy to see, but erasing the memory of what's come before is not so easily done."

Regardless of what the critics said, as 1999 and the 20th century came to an end, Julia's last three films spelled one success after another. *Stepmom* showed off her flair for drama. *Notting Hill* delighted audiences as much as *My Best Friend's Wedding* had. And with *Runaway Bride,* she finally reunited on the screen with Richard Gere.

Now Julia Roberts was poised and ready for one of the greatest successes of her entire career.

CHAPTER TEN

The 20 Million Dollar Woman

In the year 2000, both Julia Roberts and Benjamin Bratt had high-profile movies in the theaters. She was the star of an unconventional drama known as *Erin Brockovich* and he was seen as Madonna's love interest in *The Next Best Thing*. When Julia was asked how it felt seeing her boyfriend up on the screen kissing another woman—Madonna no less—she quick-wittedly quipped, "If you have to watch your boyfriend roll around with somebody, it might as well be an icon."

The evolution of the film *Erin Brockovich* is a fascinating one in itself. Just by chance, film producer Carla Santos Shamberg was at her chiropractor's office when the chiropractor told her about another one of her patients, a woman named *Erin Brockovich*. According to Carla, "It seemed incredible that this twice-divorced woman with three young children, who had no money, no resources and no formal education, had single-handedly put this lawsuit together."

Carla told her husband, Michael Shamberg, about it and they both agreed that it would make a great movie. Michael's two production partners at Jersey Films are Danny DiVito and Stacy Sher. With that, this movie started to get off of the ground.

Instantly, Julia found the script of interest to her. "What's nice about the story is that it's about a person in a very specific situation which, early on, is also a dire one. Erin is incredibly self-assured and that is the key that enables her to prevail in all situations. She is who she is and doesn't change for anybody—which is what makes her such a remarkable individual."

Julia Roberts was at a very unique point in her career. Although some of her films had been disappointing at the box office, she was on a winning streak. She had been paid $15 million for *Notting Hill* and $17 million for starring in *Runaway Bride*. Both of those films had been big hits. Now, with *Erin Brockovich*, Julia Roberts' asking price per film was an incredible $20 million.

Roberts specifically didn't want to meet the real-life *Erin Brockovich* until she was in the middle of the film. She didn't want to end up mimicking Erin's mannerisms. As she put it, "We [she and director Steven Soderbergh] had talked about the character so much, and he had spent so much time with her, gathering information and shared so much of that with me, that he kept us apart really, until she came to the set, which was about half way through the movie. Which I think was really interesting, because ultimately I think it was wise that you're not imitating somebody. I think he didn't want that. He didn't want me to pretend to be this person, he wanted me to inhabit the concept of this person." This formula ended up working perfectly.

Julia's portrayal, just like the real-life person

she was playing, was a totally unique individual. As brought to life by Julia, she wears too much makeup. She dresses a bit too provocatively. She swears when she gets mad or frustrated and she also needs a job VERY badly. This is Erin Brockovich. When her car is hit by another driver, she needs a lawyer and she ends up being represented by Ed Masry (Albert Finney). However, once he gets her to court, her smart mouth loses her the case. When she railroads Ed into offering her a job as a file clerk in his law office, he sends her out on a little fact-finding mission, which she ends up turning into a gold mine for the company.

Amidst her office research project, she is struck with confusion when she finds medical records in with the real estate dealings of certain clients. She soon unearths evidence that California power giant, PG&E (Pacific Gas & Electric), is lying about contaminating the local water supply with deadly chromium. Even more incriminating is evidence that they lied to cover their tracks.

For the first time in her life Erin Brockovich has a job that she enjoys and her life changes because of this. She doesn't just do a good job of connecting with the people whom she is interviewing, she learns how their lives have been ruined by corporate giant PG&E and their cover-up policies.

One of the most visual aspects of Julia Robert's portrayal of Erin Brockovich was the new "front" she was displaying—namely her very exposed, and her very Wonderbra-enhanced, bust line. To become the screen version of the real-life people's rights advocate, Roberts had to dress like the character did. Instead of having breast implants, Julia relied on push-up bras and tape to give her breasts the impression that they were bigger than they were in real life. According to Julia, "I'd gone 30 years without cleavage and suddenly: Pow!"

Erin Brockovich landed in theaters in October 2000. Critics universally loved her performance in the film and they fell in love with her all over again. Anwar Brett in his review for BBC1 on-line glowingly called *Erin Brockovich* "a riveting drama, made all the more fascinating for its basis in fact. Roberts plays the role with effortless charm and gritty conviction."

In *Boxoffice Online Reviews*, Bridget Byrne raved, "Finally a movie about an individual taking on unethical big business that is worthy of being compared to Capra at his least sentimental. With Julia Roberts prov-

ing her multi-wattage worth in the title role."
She further claimed, "Roberts is stunningly
convincing and appealing in the role of this
highly individualist Everywoman, gussied
up in high heels, tiny skirts and boob-reveal-
ing tops and equipped with a courageous
mouth and a tenacious spirit."

Peter Travers in *Rolling Stone* also loved
the film. He wrote in his review, "more than
an excuse to get off by watching the highest-
paid female star in Hollywood flash her
ta-tas and talk dirty ... It's a dynamite role
and Roberts comes out blazing—tough,
tender, sexy and brashly funny."

Erin Brockovich was such an incredible
box-office hit that in January 2001, it was
anticipated that Julia would be among the
nominees for an Academy Award that year.
When they were announced Feb. 13, 2001,
the woman nominated in the category of
Best Actress included: Joan Allen for *The
Contender*, Juliette Binoche in *Chocolat*,
Ellen Burstyn for *Requiem for a Dream*,
Laura Linney in *You Can Count on Me* and
Julia Roberts for *Erin Brockovich*.

Meanwhile, one of Julia's ex-boyfriends
was having some very major personal problems and Roberts offered moral support.

Since Julia's co-star in her next film *The Mexican*, Brad Pitt, was married to *Friends* TV star Jennifer Aniston, she learned of Matthew Perry's drug dependency.

After Julia had broken up with Matthew in mid-1996, he became depressed and began wildly partying. Along the way, he developed an addiction to the painkiller Vicodin. By 1997, he had to check himself into the Hazelden Center in Minnesota. In December 2000, his TV show castmates became worried about him after he appeared jumpy and moody on the set. In January 2000, Courtney Cox, Matt LeBlanc and David Schwimmer searched Perry's dressing room and found drugs. They confronted him with it and demanded that he take immediate action. He voluntarily checked himself into therapy.

Julia telephoned him and told him that he was more than welcome to go and rest up in her New Mexico home after the treatment was over. Reportedly, he was touched by the gesture and pleased that she thought of him as a true friend.

Meanwhile, Julia and Brad Pitt were filming *The Mexican*. She and Brad had long wanted to work with each other and when this quirky project came about, they both grabbed for it.

According to Julia, "I've known Brad for a long time and we had almost worked together a few times, so when this finally happened, we both got excited. We're really comfortable around each other, so from the first day were able to get the most out of the limited amount of time we had together on-screen. We came up with this whole back story about our characters to find interesting ways to convey that these people knew each other incredibly well and have been through a lot together."

Speaking for the character of Jerry, Brad explains, "Jerry is not what you'd call 'cool,' he's just a regular guy who's in way over his head. He struggles to do the right thing in his professional life and his personal life, but the line he walks constantly trips him up. He's really hung up on fairness and it's his quest for fairness in a very unfair world that I thought was really funny."

As Samantha Barzel, Julia gets to play a character who wears all of her emotions on the outside. As she throws Jerry out of their San Fernando Valley apartment, she yells out to Jerry, "You are a selfish prick and a liar."

Jerry receives a smuggling assignment from small-time thug Bernie Nyman (Bob Balaban). He is instructed to go into Mexico to retrieve a valuable pistol known as *The*

Mexican. In addition to being famous, it is also cursed. As Jerry and Samantha split up, their stories unfold separately for most of the movie.

While in rural Mexico, Jerry gets into one scrape after another. He has the gun. He loses the gun. He steals the gun back. Things take a turn for the worse when the grandson of a mobster ends up with a bullet in him, while in Jerry's company.

Meanwhile, Samantha has packed up her Volkswagen Beetle and heads to Las Vegas. It is her plan to become a waitress and then work her way into a job as croupier in one of the casinos. While in a Vegas shopping mall, she finds herself the target of two would-be kidnappers who are working for different people. In a bathroom shootout, she ends up the captive of Leroy (James Gandolfini). Samantha confides in him that she has trouble sustaining a relationship with a man. Leroy tells her he has the same problem with the men in his life. After he admits to her that he is gay, Julia seems to lose the sense that she has been kidnapped and she begins to talk to him as a friend.

Finally, Leroy and Samantha join up with Jerry. However, when Jerry suddenly shoots Leroy, there is doubt as to who is working for whom. With the adage of "no honor among thieves" coming heavily into play, *The Mexican* pistol changes hands several times before the film is over.

When the film opened in March 2001, the critics were decidedly mixed. Lisa Schwarzbaum in *Entertainment Weekly* called *The Mexican* a "Would-be-Peckinpah, wannabe-Tarantino, could-be-Gilliam story," and pointed out about the Roberts/Gandolfini scenes, "the communication between hostage and hostage taker takes *The Mexican*, at least for a time, to an exciting place."

Merrick Morton in *The Los Angeles Times* hated *The Mexican*. "It wants ever so desperately to be successfully hip and offbeat, but it can't manage to make it happen ... A violence-prone screwball farce ... One of *The Mexican*'s lines sums up its profile: 'All I got is my wallet and an attitude.' The wallet paid for Roberts and Pitt, but the attitude wears thin awfully fast."

Likewise, Peter Travers in *Rolling Stone* longed for more of Pitt and Roberts together: "*The Mexican* pairs Brad Pitt with Julia Roberts in a dream casting coup that promises a road movie of blissful comic romance and delivers a series of dramatic dead ends ...

James Gandolfini—Mr. Tony Soprano himself—in the film's best performance ... Pitt
and Roberts don't have many scenes together ... As dumb ideas go, that one is a Hall of
Famer."

However, no amount of disdain by the
critics could dampen Julia's day when, on
Sunday, March 25, 2001, the night of the
73rd annual Academy Awards, Julia won an
Oscar for Best Actress for her portrayal in
Erin Brockovich. It was one of the most
exciting moments of her entire life.

Accepting her award that night, she was
genuinely giddy and thrilled to be bestowed
this ultimate honor. Although her acceptance
speech continued for nearly four minutes,
Julia's joy was so infectious that she was
allowed to ramble on. She looked elegant and
spectacular in her black and white gown. She
was positively beaming with excitement.

"It was just so exciting," she was later to
claim, "and I felt like I had to ride the wave, go
with the flow. If you let it overwhelm you and if
you don't relax, a night like that will be over and
you'll be saying, 'Wow, what happened? Was it
fun? Did I enjoy myself?' But Benjamin and I
had just come back from a restful holiday and
he and my sister and her husband came in, and

we all went together. The four of us just went into the night with such a spirit of fun."

She looked glamorous and like she was genuinely having a good time and enjoying every minute of it. "It was a relief to get through the night in high-heeled shoes. I mean, that's a relief!" she laughed. "I was out of my mind. To this day, Benjamin or my sister or my friends ... they just laugh at me when they remember how I was that night. It was such an out-of-body experience. Just the adrenaline alone—I have newfound respect for anybody who gets up on that stage and shows any kind of poise, because to me it was a physiological impossibility. My heart was pounding like a rabbit's."

In addition to winning the Academy Award, her performance in *Erin Brockovich* also found her being heralded in the category of the year's Best Actress by The Broadcast Film Critics Association, The Los Angeles Film Critics Association, The National Board of Review and the Screen Actors Guild. In addition, she won her third Golden Globe Award from the Foreign Press Association, in the category of Best Actress in a Drama.

At the Academy Awards presentation that fateful night in 2001, Julia was on the arm of her current boyfriend, Benjamin Bratt. The photos of her beaming a broad and genuine smile, holding her Oscar and clinging to him were seen in dozens of publications.

Almost immediately after the awards show, Julia flew off to Las Vegas to begin work on the film *Ocean's Eleven*, in which she was to co-star with George Clooney. Taking into consideration Julia's past track record of having romances with her leading men, Benjamin was leery of what could happen if Julia and George hit it off as more than just co-stars. According to one report, "Ben had been worried about Julia working with George and his fears came true—immediately. Julia and George hit it off on their first night together at a party at Las Vegas' Bellagio hotel on March 29 to celebrate Julia and two other crew members winning Oscars. By the end of the evening, Julia and George were on the dance floor together doing a dirty dancing routine that had the Fontana bar in the Bellagio steaming. Julia and George were bumping and grinding together like two strippers in a men's club— sometimes they had their hands clasped around each other's butts. Then they took off for George's private luxury villa, complete with its own pool, in the hotel. Word soon got back to Ben that Julia was spending way too much time in George's villa."

Not long after she won the Academy Award, Benjamin Bratt suddenly broke up with her. According to him, his existence with her was kind of like living in a fish bowl and he didn't necessarily like it.

Another report stated: "Julia was always struggling to be what Ben wanted and failing. She would try to cook gourmet meals but they would come out a flop. She's just not 'Susie Homemaker.' All Ben wanted was a nice girl who was there for him, who could cook and clean—and that's not Julia. No matter how hard she tried, the romance was doomed."

Regarding their relationship, Bratt was later to admit, "I wasn't so naive as to go into that relationship thinking, 'This will be an entirely normal experience.' You don't build your house in a redwood grove if you don't like shade. I experienced that living at that level of visibility is something that doesn't appeal to me. And I discovered it can't really appeal to anyone. Even she, as well as other people of that magnitude of fame, doesn't enjoy it.

"It's that mosquito that buzzes in your ear when you're trying to sleep at night. You turn the light on and you can't find it. You turn the light off and it comes back again. It's constant and ever present and it disrupts any chance of peace ... When you live your life at that level of fame, it gets beyond your control. By the time you realized it, you're stuck."

Whatever the reason for the breakup, Julia didn't seem to be, or seem to act, heartbroken for long. She instantly moved forward from her breakup with Benjamin. Moving forward, of course, meant finding herself another man.

While Julia was filming *The Mexican*, she became friendly with one of the crew working on the film. He was cameraman Danny Moder. When they met, he was married to makeup artist Vera Steinberg Moder.

Danny was there for Julia when Benjamin Bratt unceremoniously dumped her in 2001. His growing relationship with Roberts led to his filing for divorce from Vera in June of that year. However, dissolving their marriage proved to be quite a battle of wits for the pair of lovers. Less-than-cooperative, Vera made them jump through several hoops before she was to sign the final divorce papers.

According to reports, the Julia and Danny affair really heated up in May and June 2001.

She was one of the producers of a film she was helping to finance, called *Grand Champion*, and she landed him a job as a cameraman for the film. Claimed one report, "That was just a cover. The real reason she was there was to hook up with Danny. When he wasn't working, Danny and Julia were virtually inseparable."

While things were heating up in her personal life, Julia began her next film project. The film, known as *America's Sweethearts*, began as an idea by Billy Crystal. He got into contact with Peter Tolan, one of the writers of the hit film, *Analyze This*. According to Crystal, "I said I had an idea for a farce based on a famous movie star couple who had starred in many movies together that were tremendously successful. But their lives together are falling apart and on their last movie together, a scenario happens that is similar to when Liz Taylor left Eddie Fisher on *Cleopatra* and ran off with Richard Burton. From there, what would happen the next time the couple saw each other? That became the basis for this comedy."

Tolan loved the idea and proceeded to write the script with Crystal. When it was completed, one of the people it was sent to was Joe Roth of Revolution Studios. Roth recalls, "I was caught up in the tone and the humor of the screenplay. When I was done with the script I thought, 'This is funny!' If you're reading a comedy and you're laughing out loud, there's a really good chance that other people will as well. It had really great characters."

Julia Roberts liked the script for *America's Sweethearts* so much that she agreed to be one of its four stars, for the bargain price of only $15 million. With a great cast including Catherine Zeta-Jones, John Cusack, Billy Crystal and Christopher Walken, it seemed like a wonderful screwball comedy and a fun high-profile project in which to work.

America's Sweethearts begins with a montage of the hit films of famous acting couple Eddie Thomas (John Cusack) and Gwen Harrison (Catherine Zeta-Jones). They worked so well together on camera that the studio is absolutely desperate to get them back together, at least long enough to promote their final film together.

So far, the studio has spent more than $86 million on the film. However, the release date is fast approaching and not only has the studio not seen the final cut of the film, but they sense disaster. What they need is for Eddie and Gwen to get back together again—even if it is a staged reunion—to promote this film, and save the studio from a huge financial disaster.

Stanley, who played Kahmel, the hit man in *The Pelican Brief* with Julia, appears as Dave Kingman, the animated but desperate studio chief. He has just fired his head publicist, Lee Phillips (Billy Crystal). Suddenly realizing that only Phillips can mastermind the reunion of Eddie and Gwen, he begs him for his job back. Organizing a gala press weekend for the premiere, he instructs his staff to do anything it takes to entertain the press.

Since splitting up, Gwen has taken a new lover, a Spanish actor named Hector Gorganzolas (Hank Azaria). Not only is his last name synonymous with cheese, but he is a complete ham. Eddie seems to have lost his drive. To regain his sense of direction, he has handed his fate to his Wellness Guide/guru (Alan Alda).

Phillips concocts a press junket at a remote place, so that he can pull all the strings and do moment-by-moment damage control. If he can keep Eddie and Gwen together long enough for their press interviews and the screening, everyone will fall in love with "America's Sweethearts" all over again.

Gwen relies heavily upon her trusty assistant, who is her sister Kiki (Julia Roberts). Kiki has just recently lost more than 60 pounds of her girth on a successful diet and everyone who sees her comments on how good she looks. For the first time in her life, spoiled and beautiful Gwen begins to feel some competition from her own sister.

In a flashback, we get to see Julia in a "fat suit" as the more rotund version of Kiki. She looks puffy and uncomfortable, and she usually has half eaten food in her hand.

For years, Kiki has handled all of the dirty work for demanding Gwen. However, now that Gwen and Eddie are finished as a couple, it is Kiki who has her eye on him. There are several funny sequences, and the actors and their suitors jockey for position, while Lee Phillips manipulates all of them.

America's Sweethearts is very imaginative and it has some very funny moments. However, it seems to lose steam in the middle. The gags take a bit too long to set up and by the time the punchline comes, it isn't as funny as it could be. Like *Something to Talk About*, this film has a lot going for it, but emerges as entertaining fun, but never makes it all the way to evoking hysterical laughter.

When it opened in July 2001, critics pretty much hated *America's Sweethearts*—universally. According to Roger Ebert in *The Chicago Sun-Times*, "*America's Sweethearts* recycles *Singin' in the Rain* but lacks the sassy genius of that 1952 musical, which is still the best comedy ever made about Hollywood ... The movie stars Julia Roberts in the Debbie Reynolds role, Catherine Zeta-Jones as Jean Hagan, John Cusack as Gene Kelly, Billy Crystal as Donald O'Connor and Stanley Tucci as Millard Mitchell (the studio head) ... Julia Roberts is sweet and lovable, Catherine Zeta-Jones is chilly and manipulative, John Cusack is desperately heartsick and Billy Crystal is, as we'd expect, convincing as the wise-guy publicist. But the screenplay, by Crystal and Peter Tolan, is all over the map."

J. Hoberman in *The Village Voice* called it "a lackluster screwball comedy and dubious Julia Roberts vehicle" and points out "the real sweetheart, of course, is Julia Roberts, who plays Zeta-Jones' long-suffering personal assistant and sister."

Kenneth Turan in *The Los Angeles Times* found "*America's Sweethearts* delights in skewering the studio publicity machinery ... All the actors in *America's Sweethearts* do well, but they are let down by a script that loses focus as things play out and a tone that verges toward sour ... entertaining as far as it goes, but it just hasn't figured out how to go far enough."

Since her latest movie was about the movie business and the whole publicity and gossip machine, it begged the question: What did she think about being the darling of the tabloids and the gossip columns? "I feel like people are entitled to their opinions, so they can say, 'good,' 'bad' or 'indifferent,' and I pretty much pass by it all. Of course, nobody wants unkind things written about them, but it's also about how you let it affect your day. For the most part, it doesn't really have an impact on my day. I mean, in the town in New Mexico where I have my place, the paper comes out once a week. So I get to miss a lot of the day-to-day gossip," she claimed.

Also, her character in *America's Sweethearts* was someone who had lost a lot of weight. Did Julia herself ever have a weight problem? According to her, "Well, I've been bigger. And adolescence hit me with a wallop, like it does a lot of people. But, you know, I don't even think it's just about weight. A lot of factors enter into a young person's self-esteem and girls seem to grapple with it more outwardly."

According to Julia, 2001 was one of her best years yet. How did she rate her happiness level? "Whenever anyone asks me that—and they ask a lot, especially lately, I think, 'How do you measure happiness?' Because, really it's all relative. When I was 10, I was pretty happy for a 10-year-old. On a different level, on a different scope. When I got my first job or when I got my first coat off of layaway, I was happy. Boy, my feet didn't touch the ground all the way home, you know? Does layaway still exist? God, that was the best thing ever."

The relative non-success of *America's Sweethearts* and *The Mexican* couldn't diffuse the high that she was now on from having won her first Academy Award. She even weathered her split with Benjamin Bratt. Now that she had taken home Oscar and was in the arms of Danny Moder, her life was happy and harmonious. For Julia Roberts, the year 2001 made her a winner in many ways.

CHAPTER ELEVEN

Team Player

When George Clooney and Brad Pitt were signed to co-star in Steven Soderbergh's 2001 remake of the 1960s classic robbery caper, *Ocean's Eleven*, they had some very strong ideas who they wanted to co-star in it with them. They sent out a script to Roberts with a note in it. According to Clooney, "We sent a copy to Julia with $20, and said: 'We hear you get 20 a film.'"

"To work with Steven again, yeah, I would do that for 20 dollars," laughs Julia. "So, yeah, that was a huge lure for me, but I was even more pleased when I actually sat down and read the script and thought it was so great and so fun and liked my little 'bit' in it."

"She's interesting and she's a bit of a puzzle," says Julia of her *Ocean's Eleven* character, Tess. "She's more than just a girl. She's got some intrigue behind her, and some difficult crosses to bear."

During the filming of *Ocean's Eleven*, there were constant rumors about Julia being seen in and around Las Vegas in the company of George Clooney. This fueled all sorts of speculation that the two of them were involved in a hot and heavy fling. The original *Ocean's Eleven* (1960) was the ultimate Rat Pack film. It starred Frank Sinatra, Dean Martin, Peter Lawford, Sammy Davis Jr. and Joey Bishop. When he set about to make a 21st-century version of this film, it was Steven Soderbergh's challenge to keep the feel, the look and the sound as cool and hip-looking as possible.

Ocean's Eleven rounds up 10 professional swindlers who are completely unrelated and binds them together into a casino robbing team of elegant professionals. George Clooney is The Idea Man, Brad Pitt is The Pro, Matt Damon is The Rookie, Carl Reiner is The High Roller, Bernie Mac is The Inside

Man, Don Cheadle is The Basher, Shaobo Qin is The Greaseman, Eddie Jemison is The Eye in the Sky, Scott Caan and Casey Affleck are The Getaway Guys and Elliott Gould is The Bankroll. Furthermore, Andy Garcia is The Victim and Julia Roberts is The Wild Card.

The plan is to have high-roller Carl Reiner, masquerading as the mysterious Mr. Zerga, distract the guards in the safe while the others get into place. In addition, a huge boxing match is simultaneously happening at the time of the planned heist. A sudden power cut disables all of the security systems, just long enough for Danny (Clooney) and Linus (Damon) to gain access to the safe.

When Danny Ocean pulls off the heist, the big question remains, what will Tess do and which man will end up with her? Does she still have love for Danny? Or is she now in love with Terry (Garcia)?

In the role of Tess, Julia Roberts is very cool and smartly glamorous. As the curator to the casino's art collection, she plays the role with chic sophistication. A great ensemble film, *Ocean's Eleven* was a big hit with theater audiences when it was released in December 2001.

The critics had varied responses to *Ocean's*

Eleven. It seemed that they either loved it a lot or hated it a lot. In his review in *USA Today*, Mike Clark was part of the latter group when he proclaimed, "The hip factor is missing in Steven Soderbergh's more tightly crafted *Ocean's Eleven* reworking, which is fatally lighter on the two V's —vermouth and Vegas mystique—that still make 1960's Rat Pack original winningly watchable ... The original is swathed in party-time legend. The new version ends up being about banal technology ... Clooney still can't convey longing or any other kind of emotional depth on-screen and, in a movie first, Roberts looks wan and tired in her limited scenes."

On the other hand, Peter Travers in *Rolling Stone* loved it and claimed, "[Director] Soderbergh's joy is contagious ... As for Clooney, his effortless star power is a thing of beauty. He'd own the movie if Elliott Gould and Carl Reiner didn't steal every scene they're in ... The whole film is relaxed, a caper with no guns, no gore and scant use of the f-word. Soderbergh's assured style is a tonic. The laughs keep coming, down to the final credits: introducing Julia Roberts—that's funny. Forget Oscar, *Ocean's Eleven* is the coolest damned thing around."

Likewise, Roger Ebert in *The Chicago Sun-Times* found it entertaining fun. "The movie excels in its delivery of dialogue. The screenplay by Ted Griffin is elegantly epigrammatic, with dialogue that sounds like a cross between Noel Coward and a 1940s *noir* thriller," he enthusiastically raved. "Clooney and Roberts deliberately evoke the elegance of stars like Cary Grant and Ingrid Bergman ... I enjoyed it. It didn't shake me up and I wasn't much involved, but I liked it as a five-finger exercise."

Still sizzling on the big-screen, events in Julia's love life were also starting to heat up—though not in a good way. Around this time reports revealed some of the negotiating terms of Danny Moder's divorce from his wife, Vera. According to one story, Julia offered Vera a $100,000 settlement fee to hurry along the divorce—more than double Moder's $45,000 annual salary. Julia and Danny were in love, Danny was over Vera and now Vera was dragging her heels. According to the article, "Vera fumed: 'Julia's desperate to wed my man, but she knows she can't until he's divorced. I'm saying to her: 'It's not going to happen. No amount of money will make me sign those papers—not until I decide I'm ready.' "

Things got nasty between Julia and Vera

before it was over. To really make Vera mad
and to coerce the legal Mrs. Danny Moder
into finally signing the papers, Julia took one
of her white T-shirts and wrote on it in very
large black Magic Marker letters, the words:
"A Low Vera." Using a misspelled version of
the skin-care plant "aloe vera," Julia was able
to get her message across.

Then, while wearing the T-shirt, Roberts
posed for photos. Was this "A Low" move on
Julia's part? She must have thought it was a
clever way to deliver a message. She flashed
a broad smile for the cameras, betraying the
enjoyment she got from her act of willful
witchiness.

According to "an insider" close to the situation, "Julia is mad as hell at Vera and this is
her way of letting her know. She's convinced
Vera is working behind the scenes to poison
her relationship with Danny and break them
up. Julia's also convinced that she's holding up
the divorce as much as possible because she
knows Julia and Danny want to get married
as soon as it comes through." The source also
claimed that Julia had taken to wearing her
message T-shirt in public on several occasions
when she knew she would be photographed.

Reportedly, the photographs of Julia in her

"A Low Vera" shirt were not found to be very amusing by Danny's family—especially his father and his sisters. Her relationship with Danny seemed to be hitting one obstacle after another.

On May 16, 2002, Vera finally signed the divorce papers and the split was made official. In an attempt to smooth things over with Danny's family, Julia decided that she would host a celebration of Danny's freedom from Vera. It was her plan to rent accommodations for she and Danny and his father and sisters in the sunny resort town of Cabo San Lucas, Mexico. However, Danny's family reportedly declined the offer. According to one report, "The Moder family thought it was crass for Julia and Danny to celebrate after his divorce. At this point, Julia feels she just can't get a break with Danny's family. Every time she feels like she's won them over, they snub her."

However, Julia and Danny went ahead with their own south-of-the-border celebration and flew down to Cabo to party on their own. Reportedly, she was moody the entire time and perplexed as to how to repair things with his family.

Regardless of the reaction Julia received with her less-than-successful Mexican adventure, by June, there was a buzz going around that something truly big was about to happen. Julia and Danny sent out invitations to her family members (minus her brother Eric), his family and several of her close friends to come to an Independence Day celebration. According to the engraved invitation, "Theme: Midsummer's Night DreamISH meets Great Gatsby-like combined with Wild West Bohemian." Guests were flown all-expenses-paid to Julia's ranch in Taos, New Mexico, for a gala Fourth of July week celebration.

The day of July 3, 2002, Julia kept her guests busy with football, basketball, a turkey dinner—cooked by Julia herself—and lounging by the swimming pool. Suddenly at midnight, everyone was instructed to grab a chair out in the yard. They were expecting some sort of a candlelight midnight brunch. What they witnessed instead was the wedding of Julia Roberts to Danny Moder!

No one had any idea that this was going to be a wedding and not just a party. Says one of Julia's close friends, "Danny got down on one knee and said, 'In front of everyone we love, I want to know, will you marry me?' And Julia grabbed her heart and said, 'Yes, yes, yes.'

And all the guests were saying, 'Yes, yes, yes,' along with her. The canopy was billowing. It was such a magical, intimate gathering, it felt like we were eavesdropping, like we were invited to someone's secret."

It was a 20-minute ceremony and it was very untraditional. There were no flower girls in frilly dresses, no line of bridesmaids holding bouquets and no Hollywood celebrity guests. In the background there were the 13,000-foot peaks of the Sangre de Cristo Mountains. Julia wore a cotton halter dress that was pale pink with embroidery and little pearls and beads sewn to it. Danny wore a red shirt with a ruffled front and Julia had a pearled tiara-like band at the front of her hairline. There was lots of toasting and laughing and kissing.

The next day, July 4, was one big, daylong reception. Around 7 p.m., a dinner of grilled vegetables and chicken was served, and soon the party was in full swing. The only celebrity present at the event was Bruce Willis, who flew in by private jet. George Clooney was invited, but instead had to fly to Maysville, Kentucky, for the funeral of his aunt, actress/singer Rosemary Clooney. After Julia's 21-month marriage to Lyle Lovett, everyone present hoped that this one would last much longer.

Despite the fun and excitement surrounding the wedding celebration, there were some members of Danny's family who were less than happy with the arrangements. Some of his family members complained that the guest cabins on her property were not air-conditioned.

Proclaimed a wedding insider, "Julia was so angry and hurt by some of her new in-laws' reaction that she lashed out at Danny. He tried to defuse smoldering Julia, but nothing could stop her. Julia and Danny were sniping at each other even before their guests had left. At one point, Danny got fed up with Julia's angry, sullen mood and said, 'Lighten up. Relax. We'll work it out.' Julia spat back, 'Don't tell me to relax! Do something about these people.' "

According to another close source who was present at the wedding, "Julia had advised guests that her Independence Day bash would run from July 2 to July 6, and boy she wasn't kidding. The guests were run ragged by the bride and groom. They'd get up in the late afternoon and start partying all over again. By Sunday when everybody left, the only ones who didn't seem worse for the wear were the bride and groom and their hounds and horses."

Later in the month, Julia broke her silence on her "instant" wedding to Danny on the ABC-TV show *Good Morning America*. Being interviewed by Diane Sawyer, Julia referred to her new husband as "a man among men, unselfish and all-encompassing."

She proclaimed on-camera that they were meant to be together: "I hope that there are people who agree that I have done some good, kind things in my life, but to really, ultimately, stand fully in a moment of realizing that I was born to love and to be the wife of this man."

Speaking of Danny's recent divorce, Julia referred to the settlement as being "terribly complicated."

She also went on to announce that she and Danny both "want to have a family and we will have a family in due course. And whether it's a gaggle... I don't know. It'll be great."

In addition to her summer wedding, it was just weeks later that her next film was released. It was the highly experimental back-to-basics Steven Soderbergh flick, *Full Frontal*.

Soderbergh had read a series of one-act vignettes written by Comeman Hough. They met and decided to string them together. They all contained two characters and each of them had the same common denominator person in their lives. The common character they all knew was a man named Gus (David Duchovny).

Soderbergh's summation of *Full Frontal* is: "If Woody Allen moved West and dropped a lot of acid he might come up with something like this." Some of the film is done in full luxurious film stock and some of it was done with an over-the-counter consumer camera. He felt that *Ocean's Eleven* had been too safe and *Full Frontal* was a throw-the-rules-out total crapshoot.

The main story is a scenario between movie star Francesca Davis (Julia Roberts) and actor Calvin Cummings (Blair Underwood). However, their initial scenes together are actually a film within this film. She is playing a character named Catherine, who is a magazine writer, and he is playing an actor named Nicholas, whom she is interviewing.

The next couple is Carl (David Hyde Pierce), who is a magazine writer; and his wife Lee (Catherine Keener). He is feeling inadequate in life and she is preparing to leave him. They are going to attend Gus' birthday party that evening and Carl bakes a batch of hashish-laced brownies for the event. In a hurry to get to work, he leaves them on the counter and their dog licks the middle of the pan out.

Then there is Art Dean (Enrico Colantoni) who is producing a play called *The Sound and the Fuhrer* about Hitler (Nicky Katt). Art is planning an Internet blind date with Linda, who is Lee's sister.

Linda (Mary McCormack) is a masseuse. The day of the party, she arrives to give Gus a massage and he talks her into a massage with orgasmic "release." Uneasy with the situation, he bribes her into it with $500 cash. Gus gets his "release" and she ends up being able to afford a new dress for his party that evening.

As the stories intertwine, the couples interact. Lee has sex with Calvin. Carl loses his job and comes home to find his dog stoned on brownies. When the vet arrives (Soledad St. Hilaire), she and Carl eat some of the un-dog-licked brownies.

A rambling, jump-cutting film that has the look of real stars doing an NYU film student's senior project, *Full Frontal* is not for everyone. This experimental cinema of non-sequiturs was one which either fascinated audiences or caused them to yawn. Made on a shoestring budget of $20 million, *Full Frontal* was an experiment that fell flat at the box office.

Full Frontal opened in movie theaters in August 2002. Several critics didn't know what to make of it. Others hated it. And some loved it. Writing for *Entertainment Weekly*, Lisa Schwarzbaum snidely commented, "*Full Frontal* is a tricky novelty item: The director himself has variously described it as an 'experiment,' an 'exercise,' and a 'sketch.' ... If *Ocean's Eleven* was a high-priced banquet of popular guys toasting one another's hard-earned coolness in a pointless caper, *Full Frontal* is the after-party. It's a low-budget, late-night game of strip poker hosted by a really smart guy who still can't quite believe how much the popular kids now want to sit at his table."

Ann Hornaday of *The Washington Post* wrote, "*Full Frontal* has to do with one 24-hour period in the lives of all of these characters—the artists, writers, posers and walking wounded who glide through Los Angeles like so many sharks and pilot fish ... With sex, lies and videotape, Soderbergh seemed to be knocking on Hollywood's door to get in. Now, as a full-fledged insider, he seems to have made *Full Frontal* to catch a breath of fresh air. More power to him. This movie seems to have been conceived primarily for the benefit of the filmmaker, his friends and subscribers to *Entertainment Weekly*."

And Roger Ebert of *The Chicago Sun-Times*

pointed out, "*Full Frontal*, a film so amateur-ish that only the professionalism of some of the actors makes it watchable. This is the sort of work we expect from a film school student with his first digital camera, not from the gifted director of *Traffic* and *Out of Sight* ... The movie within the movie stars Julia Roberts as a journalist interviewing Blair Underwood; shots that are supposed to be this movie are filmed in lush 35mm and only serve to make us yearn for the format as we see the other scenes, in digital ... There is a scene in *Full Frontal* where a character comes to a tragic end while masturbating. That could symbolize the method and fate of this film."

Julia Roberts had her hands full for the moment. Not only did she have a new husband that she had pursued and won, she also had three new films in the works. She was at the top of her game and she wasn't about to pause for a moment.

CHAPTER TWELVE

That Mona Lisa Smile

While her career was progressing well, there were all sorts of reports of trouble in paradise in the life of Julia and Danny. In the fall of 2001, photographers snapped photos of the duo having a very public argument outside her Gramercy Park apartment in New York City. Apparently, they were packing up their vehicle for a weekend out of the city. In addition to the unmistakable photographs, an eyewitness claimed: "She was staring at Danny angrily and hissing for him to speed it up, because she wanted to leave as soon as possible. But he made it clear he wouldn't put up with any tantrums. He glared back a her then waved his hand down the street, motioning for her to take the dog for a walk before they left."

According to a friend quoted in that same article, "The honeymoon is definitely over. Julia's wildly jealous and a control freak, and she's on Danny's case all the time."

Another point of disappointment for Julia was her inability to become pregnant. She had stated many times that she longed to become a mother, but her attempts with Danny were not yielding results. According to press reports in late 2002 and early 2003, they were not ruling out the possibility of adopting a baby.

According to an insider, "Julia has contacted a number of different agencies representing several different countries. These include China, Romania, Russia and Cambodia— they're not limiting themselves to one particular nationality. They're so excited that they've already looked for furniture for the nursery and hit expensive stores in Malibu like '98% Angel' to shop for baby clothes and toys for the tot." Although this might be true, "the stork" never seemed to get the message that Julia Roberts was shopping around for a new role in real-life: motherhood.

Even though she was busy finishing up shooting the film *Mona Lisa Smile*, in December 2002 Julia was back on the big screen in *Confessions of a Dangerous Mind*. It wasn't a film in which she starred, but she had a recurring role in the film. The reason that she was asked to be in the movie—along with Drew Barrymore and George Clooney—was that it was the first film directed by her buddy Clooney.

Confessions of a Dangerous Mind is a totally quirky film that is part biography, part fantasy and part documentary. It is the life story of a show business idea man named Chuck Barris. As a young man Barris penned the rock 'n' roll hit song, *Palisades Park*, which was recorded by Freddy "Boom Boom" Cannon. In the late 1960s, Barris launched a new career as a game show creator and host and was the mastermind behind the hugely successful TV series *The Dating Game* and *The Gong Show*. Like a modern day P.T. Barnum, Barris insisted that people will do anything for 15 minutes of television fame, even if it means making a complete idiot out of themselves.

The even more surreal subplot that fuels *Confessions of a Dangerous Mind* is that Barris asserts that he was once employed by the CIA as a government "hit man." To make the film even more surreal, celebrities like Dick Clark and Betsy Palmer appear in documentary footage, discussing the real life Barris' odd life and career.

Most interesting is the fact that this film marks George Clooney's directorial debut. The cast includes relatively unknown Sam Rockwell as Barris. Drew Barrymore plays Chuck's long-suffering but eternally optimistic girlfriend, Penny. Clooney plays the role of the CIA agent who first approaches Barris to accept high-risk secret operations for the U.S. government.

Julia Roberts plays a role which recurs throughout the movie. She is the mysterious agent known as Patricia. Her first scene is in a Helsinki, Finland, bar. She wears a huge wide-brimmed hat. She looks different every time she shows up in the film. In a West Berlin rathskeller she is disguised in a blond wig. Wishing Barris luck on one of his assignments, she says to him, "Kill for me, baby!"

When it was released in theaters in January 2003, *Confessions of a Dangerous Mind* was met with mixed reviews. In *The Los Angeles Times*, Kenneth Turan hated this film so much that his review of it was entitled, "Confessions: Quick! Somebody get the gong!" According to him, "George Clooney's first effort behind the camera was doubtless more stimulating to direct than it will be for audiences to watch ... Barris' triumphs and his crises mean the same to us: Zero ... Julia Roberts as a rival assassin, encouraging a nudge-nudge, wink-wink style that stumbles all over itself in its zeal to be arch and hip."

Desson Howe in *The Washington Post* rather liked *Confessions of a Dangerous Mind*. He pointed out, "Chuck Barris oversaw such hit TV shows as *The Dating Game* while also performing dangerous missions for the CIA. He claims to have killed 33 people. Talk about multitasking! ... the movie's a darkly enjoyable roller-coaster ride ... [Director] Clooney and [screenplay writer Charlie] Kaufman have taken Barris' autobiography at its word and gone for it all the way."

And Peter Travers in *Rolling Stone* found it favorable as well, pointing out, "How does George Clooney handle his first job as a

director? He makes a game of it ... Clooney
shows real verve with the actors ... Julia
Roberts, without a movie to carry, plays it fun
and loose as a spy out of Chuck's fantasies.
Clooney fashions a style all his own: Visceral,
vital and churning with off-the-wall ideas.
That's what makes you want to see Clooney
direct again. You can feel his joy in it."

On March 23, 2003, Julia Roberts was on
hand in Hollywood at the 75th Annual
Academy Awards. Looking beautiful on stage
at the Kodak Theater, Julia presented the
award for Best Cinematography to Conrad L.
Hall for his work on the film, *Road to Perdition*.
She also participated in a big gala toward the
end of the show, with an all-star collection of
past winners including Barbra Streisand,
Olivia de Havilland, Sean Connery, Mickey
Rooney, Luise Rainer and dozens more.

By this time, Julia was finished with *Mona
Lisa Smile*. Not only starring in the film, Julia
is also the executive producer. It is about a
Berkeley graduate in 1953 who is very free-
spirited. When she becomes a teacher at
famed Midwest women's college Wellesley,
sparks fly. Directed by Mike Newell, Julia
Roberts plays the lead role of Katherine
Watson. The supporting cast includes Kirsten

Dunst, Julia Stiles, Maggie Gyllenhaal, Ginnifer Goodwin, Dominic West, James Callahan and Marcia Gay Harden.

In early 2003, it was announced that George Clooney and director Steven Soderbergh were already mounting the sequel to *Ocean's Eleven*—the aptly titled *Ocean's Twelve* to be filmed and released in 2004.

There was also talk in 2003 about Julia teaming up with *Sex & the City* creator Darren Star to bring Tracy Quan's book, *Diary of a Manhattan Call Girl—A Nancy Chan Novel*, to the big screen. It is projected to be a feature with Julia playing a prostitute in it. Julia's own Shoelace Productions tapped Darren Star to adapt the book to a screenplay.

For more than 15 years now, Julia Roberts has been recognized as a major movie star. There is a certain pressure on Julia to always look her best when she is in public. Does she enjoy getting all dressed up for a Hollywood event? "If I go out to a premiere, I try to look nice. I try to get my hair done, put on lipstick, all that kind of stuff," she explains. "But I'm not going to make myself nuts. I go out to the grocery store in a pair of jeans and my hair in a knot on the top of my head. I think Joan Crawford used to say that she never went anywhere without the full head-to-toe presentation. I could never be that person."

She professes that she is not a full-time clotheshorse. "I'm certainly interested in fashion. I like pretty clothes just like any girl. But I'm never going to be the girl where everyone's saying, 'Oooh, I can't wait to see what she wears next.' That's just not me. Sometimes, if I have to dress up weekend after weekend, it gets to the point where I feel like, 'Oh, my God, I can't pull it together one more time. I can't do this.' " And, do you know, I've heard about some people who will actually have a run-through—hair, makeup, gown—a few days before a big event? I'm kind of fascinated by that, but would never go there."

Although she's been in the business for quite a while, she still winces at bad reviews for her films. "Professional criticism bothers me more than the personal stuff," she claims. "When people comment negatively about the way I look or dress, it doesn't really bother me. It would be different if my best girlfriend said I looked terrible or I looked too thin or she didn't like my dress. Then I'd really be hurt. But not when it's some person whose name I don't even know."

Being bright and cheery at the drop of a hat

doesn't always come easy for Julia. According to her, "There's nothing worse than being in a bad mood when you're supposed to be buoyant. Having to laugh when you don't feel like it is like swimming against the tide. That's the worst thing in the world. Even fake crying is better than fake laughing."

Is there a pressure on her to remain thin? "I've never felt that pressure," she claims. "I mean, I'm responsible to be healthy and fit, and if I turn into a big fat frog, then I've done that to myself. But as far as being thought of as pretty, well, of course I'd rather people think I'm pretty than a dogface, but it's not something that I am responsible for."

Does she feel better in a relationship? "It depends on the relationship," she reveals. "In general, I think I'd rather be a free gal, except I now understand—at long last—that in a great relationship you can still maintain all the things that make you happy. You don't have to take water out of the boat and put different water in. You don't have to evaporate. I think a lot of my misunderstanding of relationships was in thinking that I had to evaporate to be someone's girlfriend. But I have no regrets about any relationship I've had, even the worst-case scenarios. Because if you can figure out why it all happened, then it serves an invaluable purpose."

What is it that really peeves Julia Roberts? According to her, "Pettiness, narrow-mindedness, stupidity. I hate when people don't think before they say or do something. And I was really pissed off when the press labeled me a notorious drug addict. Notorious? That was probably the most hurtful thing that's ever been written. My mom was going, 'What's happening? Look how thin she is. She's a drug addict and she's horrible.' It really hurt. I was like, 'Don't pin that on me. I'm better than that.' Not only do I not want people thinking I'm a drug addict, I don't even know how anybody can do drugs and still work. If I don't get seven hours of sleep, I can hardly function. I have to have all my wits about me."

If Julia is hooked on anything, she's hooked on bringing interesting characters to life on the screen. "I'm not making movies to be famous. I'm not making movies to be rich. It's more like I say, 'OK, I like this girl and I think I can be her for the next four months. I think I can make an interesting her.' And that's a good reason to do it." According to her, she is in the film business for the long haul. "I'd like to have the shelf life of one of those Hostess cupcakes, those pink ones with the white on it. That should be about 38 more years."

She is also more interested in living in the present than examining her past or projecting herself into the future. As she puts it, "I would rather just be present, because this moment in my life will never come again. Just think how you work to get someplace and how when you get there, you're suddenly on to the next thing."

Julia is very happy with the person she has grown up to become. She is very much in control of her own life and she is happy with the decisions she has made. "I used to think I was weird. Now I think I'm just interesting," she says.

What is it that attracts people to Julia Roberts? According to the actress herself, "I think if anything, it has to do with a sense of fun that I project. I think people respond to a feeling of: 'Oh, she looks like she's having fun. She looks like she's having a good time.' And maybe they appreciate that—I look like I'm actually where I want to be."

What would Julia do if her acting career suddenly came to a crashing end? "There are so many things I'd like to do. I wouldn't even know where to begin. I love these documentaries I've made about endangered wildlife. So many things interest me. I'd probably go back to school."

A lot of people don't realize that Julia is very well-read and that she has many interests outside of show business. "I love to read," she claims. And I do subscribe to the idea that knowledge is power ... but I also believe in the adage that the more I know, the more I realize I don't know. And, with the documentaries ... they're so exciting, it's such a great adventure to go off with the people I make these films with, and to be able to go forth into a brand-new world."

What is it she looks forward to? "I don't project beyond tomorrow. I never do." However, she does always have her eye on self-improvement. "I hope I'm becoming a better person and becoming a grown-up. But I think I'm still pretty simple and I still have the same value structure that I've always had. I'm just changing in that I want to be more, to be better—I want to be a better friend. I want to be a better cook. But I don't think I'm a different person."

She is much more self-assured in the way that she carries herself these days. She reveals, "I used to be so scared to be impolite or I felt that if somebody asked me a question, then I had a responsibility to answer it—regardless of how inappropriate the question was. Now I've realized that I have a right as a person to share only what I feel comfortable sharing and that it doesn't make me a bad person if I say, 'I don't choose to answer that.'"

With regard to having children, she proclaimed, "Oh, absolutely. I definitely want kids." However, she has also revealed, "If I'm married when that happens, terrific. If I'm not, well that's fine, too."

Apparently, having a baby was on Julia's mind in 2003. Reportedly, she had been visiting fertility clinics to see if she could hasten things along. Since finishing filming *Mona Lisa Smile* in January 2003, the timing seemed right. After all, if she wanted to have children, she figured that at the age of 35, she had best get moving with this project.

After they were married, Julia and Danny bought a house in a very trendy section of Venice, California. Since the houses were so close together, they purchased two lots of adjacent property. It was their intention to build a six-foot high fence around the house for privacy. However, the city wouldn't approve a fence that tall. Because of this, they were entertaining the idea of selling the house.

Already in early 2003, the press reported rumblings about Julia Roberts' marriage to Danny Moder being on shaky ground. Like the *Runaway Bride* that she once played on the big screen, would she once again flee her second marriage as quickly as her first? Only time would tell.

With a track record as a "hit and run" lover, Julia Roberts is very fickle in real life. Perhaps there is no man who can hold her for long. Would she remain with Danny? Or would she break up with him and just remain friends, like she did with Lyle Lovett? Never one to stand still, Julia Roberts' roller coaster love life continues to evolve and unfold.

Although she has had an adventure-filled and checkered past when it comes to interpersonal relationships, one thing has remained a constant in her life and that is her career. Julia Roberts is one of the most determined and driven women in show business. No personal disappointments can get in the way for her. At the apex of her acting career, she isn't about to slow down. Julia has such incredible versatility and such across-the-board appeal, there is nearly no role that she cannot tackle.

She is known for her smile and her radiant personality. Even in some of her gloomier films, like *Mary Reilly* and *Michael Collins*, whenever she is on the screen, she is all that one can watch. She is into fairness, ecological issues and human rights. Like the title character she played in *Erin Brockovich*, Julia Roberts is not afraid to roll up her sleeves and get involved in a cause in real life. However, she will also be forever known as the incredible, appealing star of *Pretty Woman*. Her charm, her vulnerability and her determination make her an appealing and unique film star. There is no one quite like Julia Roberts.

APPENDICES

FILMS BY JULIA ROBERTS

Blood Red (filmed in 1986, released in 1988)

Firehouse (1987)

Satisfaction (1988)

Baja Oklahoma (1988)

Mystic Pizza (1988)

Steel Magnolias (1989)

Pretty Woman (1990)

Flatliners (1990)

Sleeping With the Enemy (1991)

Dying Young (1991)

Hook (1991)

The Player (1992)

The Pelican Brief (1993)

Ready to Wear (1994)

I Love Trouble (1994)

Something to Talk About (1995)

Mary Reilly (1996)

Michael Collins (1996)

Everyone Says I Love You (1996)

My Best Friend's Wedding (1997)

Conspiracy Theory (1997)

Stepmom (1998)

Notting Hill (1999)

Runaway Bride (1999)

Erin Brockovich (2000)

The Mexican (2001)

America's Sweethearts (2001)

Ocean's Eleven (2001)

Full Frontal (2002)

Confessions of a Dangerous Mind (2002)

Mona Lisa Smile (2003)

TELEVISION APPEARANCES

Crime Story playing "Tracy" in episode #1.19: "The Survivor" Feb. 13, 1987

Miami Vice playing "Polly Wheeler" in episode #4.22: "Mirror Image" May 6, 1988

The Howard Stern Show (1994) playing herself

Inside the Actors Studio (1994)

Friends playing "Susie Moss" in episode #2.12: "The One After the Super Bowl" Jan. 28, 1996

Murphy Brown playing herself in episode #10.21: "Never Can Say Goodbye: Part 1" May 18, 1998

Murphy Brown playing herself in episode #10.22: "Never Can Say Goodbye: Part 2" May 18, 1998

Sesame Street playing herself, Dec. 28, 1998

Law & Order playing "Katrina Ludlow" in episode #9.20: "Empire" May 5, 1999

Nature playing herself in episode: "Wild Horses of Mongolia with Julia Roberts" Oct. 22, 2000

Revealed with Jules Asner (2001) playing herself in episode: "Julia Roberts Revealed"

America—A Tribute to Heroes (Telethon Broadcast) 2001

ACTING AWARDS & NOMINATIONS

1989

Nominee: Best Supporting Actress, *Steel Magnolias*, Oscar/Academy Awards

1990

Winner: Best Supporting Actress, *Steel Magnolias*, Golden Globe

1990

Nominee: Best Actress, *Pretty Woman*, Oscar/Academy Awards, British Academy Awards

1991

Winner: Best Actress in a Comedy or Musical, *Pretty Woman*, Golden Globe

1997

Nominee: Best Actress in a Comedy or Musical, *My Best Friend's Wedding*, Golden Globe

1997

Nominee: Best Actress in a Comedy or Musical, *My Best Friend's Wedding*, Golden Globe

1999

Nominee: Best Actress in a Comedy or Musical, *Notting Hill*, Golden Globe

2000

Winner: Best Actress, *Erin Brockovich*, Oscar/Academy Awards, Golden Globe Awards, British Academy Awards, Broadcast Film Critics Association, L.A. Film Critics Association, National Board of Review, Screen Actors Guild

ESCALATING PER-PICTURE SALARY

Mystic Pizza (1988)	$50,000
Steel Magnolias (1989)	$90,000
Pretty Woman (1990)	$300,000
Flatliners (1990)	$500,000
Sleeping With the Enemy (1991)	$1 million
Dying Young (1991)	$3 million
Hook (1991)	$7 million
The Pelican Brief (1993)	$8 million
Mary Reilly (1996)	$10 million
My Best Friend's Wedding (1997)	$12 million
Conspiracy Theory (1997)	$12 million
Notting Hill (1999)	$15 million
Runaway Bride (1999)	$17 million
Erin Brockovich (2000)	$20 million
The Mexican (2001)	$20 million
America's Sweethearts (2001)	$15 million
Ocean's Eleven (2001)	$10 million
Confessions of a Dangerous Mind (2002)	$250,000 (scale)

BOYFRIENDOGRAPHY

DYLAN WALSH . . . . *New York waiter*
Julia dated him from 1986 to 1987.

LIAM NEESON . . . . *actor*
Julia met him while filming *Satisfaction* and
they were together from 1987 to 1988.

DYLAN McDERMOTT . . . . *actor*
Julia's co-star in *Steel Magnolias*. They met in
1988 and were engaged. She called off the
engagement in 1989.

KIEFER SUTHERLAND . . . . *actor*
Met Julia when they co-starred in *Flatliners*
in 1989. They were engaged to be married on
June 14, 1991. She called off the wedding just
days before it was to take place.

JASON PATRIC . . . . *actor*
They were together from 1991 to December 1992.

DANIEL DAY-LEWIS . . . . *actor*
Their short-lived affair lasted from January to
May 1993.

LYLE LOVETT . . . . *singer*
Co-stars of two films, *The Player* and *Ready to
Wear*. They were married June 27, 1993, after
a month-long courtship, and separated in
March 1995.

ETHAN HAWKE . . . . *actor*
Julia sought solace with Ethan right after her
marriage to Lyle crumbled in 1994.

MARIO FONTANELLA . . . .*gondolier*
Julia was ferried about Venice by Mario while
she was in Italy to film *Everyone Says I Love
You* in September 1995.

LORENZO SALVAN . . . .*bodyguard*
Julia also met him in Italy amidst the filming
of *Everyone Says I Love You* and traveled with
him to Paris and the Alps in 1995.

PAT MANOCCHIA . . . .*health club owner*
Julia dated him on and off in 1995 and from
July to December 1996. Also, in 1997 there
was talk of wedding bells for the duo, but it
never transpired.

MATTHEW PERRY . . . .*actor*
They met when Julia guest starred on the TV
show *Friends*. They dated from January 1996
until July 1996.

ROSS PARTRIDGE . . . .*bartender*
Dated from December 1996 to November 1997.

BENJAMIN BRATT . . . .*actor*
Dated from November 1997 to May 2001. He
broke up with her because he hated his
personal life being in the spotlight .

DANNY MODER . . . .*cameraman*
They met while Julia was filming *The
Mexican*. They were married July 4, 2002.

<u>ACKNOWLEDGEMENTS</u>

The author would like to thank the following people for their assistance and encouragement in writing this book:

—Bob & Mary Bego
—Angela Bowie
—Trippy Cunningham
—Jerry George
—John Klinger
—Marcy MacDonald
—George Vissichelli
—Val Virga

BIBLIOGRAPHY

The following magazines and newspapers have
been utilized in the research and source material
for this book:

The Anchorage Press
Austin Chronicle
Biography
The Boston Globe
Box Office Magazine
Boxoffice Online
The Chicago Sun-Times
The Deseret News, Salt Lake City
Entertainment Weekly
Esquire
Eye Weekly
Globe
Good Housekeeping
GQ
Harper's Bazaar
In Touch
Ladies' Home Journal
Mademoiselle
McCall's
The National Enquirer
The New York Times
Newsweek
People
Playboy

Premiere
Redbook
Rolling Stone
The San Francisco Chronicle
The San Francisco Examiner
Seattle Times
Star
Sunday News, Australia
Tucson Weekly
US
Vanity Fair
Vogue
The Washington Post

Books referenced include:
—*Leonard Maltin's 1998 Movie & Video Guide*, Leonard Maltin, 1997, Signet/Penguin Books, New York City
—*Video Movie Guide 2001*, Mick Martin & Marsha Porter, 2000, Ballantine Books, New York City